Practical Law for Jail and Prison Personnel

By the National Institute for
Citizen Education in the Law

From The National Institute for Citizen Education in the Law
and West Publishing Company

Practical Law for Jail and Prison Personnel

By the National Institute for
Citizen Education in the Law

Margaret Fisher
Adjunct Professor of Law
University of Puget Sound School of Law

Edward O'Brien
Adjunct Professor of Law
Georgetown University Law Center

David T. Austern
Adjunct Professor of Law
Georgetown University Law Center

West Publishing Company
St. Paul ◆ New York ◆ Los Angeles ◆ San Francisco

Copyeditor: Susan C. Jones
Cover Design: Peter Thiel
Cover Image: Bill Powers/Frost Publishing Group, Ltd.

Photo Credits
Note: Unless listed separately below, photos on each chapter-
opening spread also appear within the corresponding chapter text.
Please refer to text page numbers for credits of photos shown on chapter-opening spreads.

Robert V. Eckert, Jr., EKM-Nepenthe: pp. 120, 149.
Frost Publishing Group, Ltd.: pp. 53, 159.
Minnesota Department of Corrections: p. 75.
Tony O'Brien/Frost Publishing Group, Ltd.: pp. 29, 44, 56, 100, 133.
Bill Powers/Frost Publishing Group, Ltd.: pp. 37, 47, 88, 101, 104, 106,
  113, 122, 128, 135, 141, 169.
Wilbert Rideau/Frost Publishing Group, Ltd.: p. 151.
James L. Shaffer: pp. 8, 93, 154.

Library of Congress Cataloging-in-Publication Data

Fisher, Margaret.
  Practical law for jail and prison personnel.

  Second ed. of: Practical law for correctional
personnel/National Street Law Institute.
  Bibliography: p.
  Includes index.
  1. Correctional law—United States. 2. Correctional
personnel—Legal status, laws, etc.—United States.
I. O'Brien, Edward L. II. Austern, David.
III. National Street Law Institute. Practical law for
correctional personnel. IV. Title.
KF9728.F57 1987   344.73'035   86–23406
ISBN 0–314–26415–9 347.30435

∞

Contents

CHAPTER 5 ◆ The Role of Jail and Prison Personnel in a Typical Civil Lawsuit 139

Acknowledgments

The authors and the National Institute for Citizen Education in the Law (NICEL) would like to thank the National Institute of Corrections (NIC) for funding a grant that assisted us in adapting previously developed materials for teaching law to nonlawyers into this present curriculum for correctional personnel. Grants from NIC also made it possible to field-test the materials in the District of Columbia, Virginia, Louisiana, and at NIC's National Jail Center and the National Academy of Corrections in Boulder, Colorado. In particular, Allen Breed, Craig Dobson, Gary Bowker, Bill Wilkey, Paul Katsampes, Dan Tabizon, Nelda Leon and Alfredo Murphy, all of NIC, have been very helpful in this effort.

Many professionals in the field of corrections have given considerable guidance in the development of these materials. Most noteworthy assistance has come from Richard Crane, former General Counsel, Louisiana Department of Corrections and now Vice President and General Counsel, Corrections Corporation of America, and a member of NICEL's Advisory Committee. Richard Crane recognized a very real need for this type of training and consequently has included a discussion of it in the American Correctional Association's conferences on corrections law, which he conducted nationwide. He also gave initial guidance on the overall format and later provided excellent detailed comments on drafts. Finally, he made it possible for the materials to be field-tested with personnel from the Louisiana Department of Corrections. Richard Crane's successor at the Correctional Law Project, and now Director of Training of the New York City Police Department, Jess Maghan, has also strongly supported our endeavors.

Thanks should also go to the American Correctional Association's Committee on training and correctional law—in particular, to Robert Martin, Cherry Scott, John Murphy, John Cocoras, Tommy Cave, Eugene Barkin, and Anthony Travisano, who gave direction to the general format. Valuable comments have also been received from William C. Collins and William Taylor of the American Correctional Association, and Eugene Barkin of our Advisory Committee.

This revision and update has benefitted from comments and suggestions again from Richard Crane and also from Joseph Marchese of the New York State Commission on Corrections; Michael Gilbert, Corrections Consultant; and Janet Kottman-Gregory, a corrections attorney and trainer in legal issues. Valuable assistance in editing and proofreading has been provided by Nancy Switkes, NICEL's Assistant Director for Publications.

Our publisher, West Publishing Company, has also been very helpful, recognizing the need for these materials and providing excellent suggestions and assistance. Special thanks go to Carole Grumney for her editorial assistance and to Nancy Roth who has served as production editor for this edition.

Ellen Cochrane developed the glossary and her efforts are greatly appreciated. Our entire support staff deserves the largest share of our gratitude for their efforts in the preparation of these materials.

Margaret Fisher
Edward L. O'Brien
David T. Austern

Assistance to Instructors of Jail and Prison Personnel

NICEL has developed this text and its accompanying Instructor's Manual to form the basis of pre-service or in-service training in law for correctional personnel or for use in other college courses in corrections law. NICEL has developed training programs in which its staff and consultants work with trainers (attorneys and/or non-lawyer professional trainers) who then conduct legal training programs for correctional personnel. The staff and consultants also conduct training for states and localities on a consulting basis.

NICEL has also published curriculum materials and general law courses designed for youths and adults either in or outside of institutions, in schools, and in community-education settings. The principal book for these courses is *Street Law: A Course in Practical Law,* Third Edition, 1986 (West Publishing Company), which covers Introduction to Law, Criminal, Consumer, Family, Housing and Individual Rights Law and is accompanied by a Teacher's Manual. NICEL also has other books and audio-visual materials.

For further information on these training programs, courses, and materials, contact: National Institute for Citizen Education in the Law, 25 E Street, N.W., Suite 400, Washington, D.C. 20001. Telephone: (202) 662–9620.

The National Institute for Citizen Education in the Law

The National Institute for Citizen Education in the Law (NICEL) is an outgrowth of a Georgetown University program started in 1971 in which law students teach law courses in District of Columbia high schools, in juvenile and adult correctional institutions, and in a number of community-based programs.

The Institute was created to promote increased opportunities for citizen education in law. It is involved in course development, teacher training, and program replication. Other NICEL activities include providing technical assistance and curriculum materials to law schools, school systems, departments of corrections, juvenile justice agencies, bar associations, legal service organizations, community groups, state and local governments, and others interested in establishing law-related education programs.

Other publications of NICEL include the following:

Street Law, A Course in Practical Law (1986, Third Edition)
Great Trials in American History (1985)
Excel in Civics (1985)
Current Legal Issues Filmstrip Series II (1985)
Family Law: Competencies in Law and Citizenship (1984)

Street Law: Mock Trial Manual (1984)

Current Legal Issues Filmstrip Series I (1984)

Consumer Law: Competencies in Law and Citizenship (1983)

Street Law Filmstrip Series (1983)

Law and the Consumer (1982)

For further information or assistance, please contact

National Institute for Citizen Education in the Law

25 E Street N.W.

Suite 400

Washington, D.C. 20001

(202) 662–9620

NATIONAL ADVISORY COMMITTEE

David R. Brink, Chairman
Dorsey & Whitney
Minneapolis, Minnesota

Grace Baisinger
National PTA
Washington, D.C.

Richard Bastiani
Syva Company
Palo Alto, California

Lowell R. Beck
National Association of
  Independent Insurers
Des Plaines, Illinois

Jane A. Couch
National Public Radio
Washington, D.C.

Richard Crane
Corrections Corporation of
  America
Nashville, Tennessee

Lawrence Dark
American Red Cross
Washington, D.C.

Elisabeth T. Dreyfuss
Cleveland-Marshall College of
  Law
Cleveland, Ohio

Gretchen Dykstra
Edna McConnel Clark
  Foundation
New York, New York

Thomas W. Evans
Mudge Rose Guthrie Alexander
  & Ferdon
New York, New York

C. Hugh Friedman
University of San Diego Law
  School
San Diego, California

Brenda Girton
Sears, Roebuck & Co.
Washington, D.C.

Frances Haley
National Council for the Social
  Studies
Washington, D.C.

Practical Law for Jail and Prison Personnel

By the National Institute for
Citizen Education in the Law

CHAPTER 1

Introduction to Law

WHY JAIL AND PRISON PERSONNEL
SHOULD STUDY LAW

When may jail and prison personnel use force to break up a fight among inmates? What risks or *liabilities* * are involved in using such force? What can be done if an inmate threatens an officer's family? Will the Department of Corrections always supply an attorney to represent personnel who are sued by an inmate? Suppose officers or administrators are sued by an inmate and the jury awards money *damages* against them. Will the Department of Corrections pay the *judgment,* or must it come out of the employees' salaries?

The list is endless, and we probably could pose hundreds of other questions about the rights and liabilities of correctional personnel. The point is obvious: Jail and prison personnel have positions that require daily decisions about people and their rights, and a knowledge of the law is necessary for performing the job effectively. Jail and prison personnel are also a part of the criminal justice system, and some knowledge of criminal law, criminal procedure, and post-conviction relief is essential.

Sometimes a knowledge of the law provides information that is both useful and important. For instance, do you know that under the Public

---

* The first time a legal term is introduced in this book, it will appear in italics and be defined in Appendix A, the Glossary.

Safety Officers' Act of 1976, depending on the circumstances, the family of an officer killed in the line of duty *may* be eligible for payment of $50,000? Jail and prison officers can enjoy other benefits without being killed or injured. Rights are protected by laws, and a knowledge of those laws is the best way to insure the full benefit of those rights.

In the past, correctional personnel generally have been given very superficial training in the law—perhaps as little as one or two hours of training. We believe more thorough training is essential. Most police officers, sheriffs, and other law enforcement personnel are given some legal training. Correctional personnel should also be trained in the law; indeed, it may be more essential for those working in *jails* and *prisons* to know the law than it is for other law enforcement officers.

Finally, although some areas of the law are not subject to frequent change, corrections law, perhaps more than any other area of the law, has changed remarkably in the past fifteen years. It continues to change and develop in new and different directions; knowing what the law is and what it may become is important.

WHAT IS LAW?

The answer to this question has troubled people for many years. In fact, an entire field of study, *jurisprudence,* is devoted to answering this question. Depending on one's point of view, there are many definitions of "the law," but for our purposes, law is best understood as that set of rules or regulations by which a particular group or community regulates the conduct of people within it.

Using this definition, many questions arise.

- Where do laws come from? Who makes the law?
- Do we need laws?
- Are all laws written?
- Can laws change? If so, how?
- What is the difference between laws and morals?
- Are all laws fair? Should we be permitted to ignore unfair laws?

Our legal system is influenced by traditional ideas of "right and wrong." Thus, most people would condemn murder, regardless of what the law said. On the other hand, everything that someone considers immoral is not illegal. For example, lying to a friend may be immoral but would rarely be illegal. The point is that every society has recognized the need for some law. These laws may not have been written, but even primitive people had rules regulating group conduct. Without laws, there would be confusion, fear, and panic. This is not to say that all of our existing laws are "fair" or even good, but imagine how people might take advantage of one another without some set of rules.

Problem 1

Make a list of the things jail and prison personnel do during a normal shift in a correctional institution (e.g., sort mail, take count, feed the residents, clean up, etc.). Next to each item in the list, indicate whether there are any laws affecting this activity. Are these federal, state, or other types of laws?

It is the application of laws to particular situations that concerns lawyers and the courts. Regardless of how simply stated or obvious the law in question—for instance, the *statute* involved in the next problem is only thirteen words long—applying the law is frequently difficult. As bizarre as it may seem, the facts described below are taken from an actual case.

The Case of the Shipwrecked Sailors

While working as sailors on an ocean-going oil tanker, three young men were cast adrift in a life raft after their ship floundered and sank in the Atlantic Ocean. The ship went down so suddenly that there was no time to send out an S.O.S., and, as far as the three sailors knew, they were the only survivors. In the boat, they had no food or water, and they had no fishing gear or other equipment for getting food from the ocean.

After recovering from the initial shock of the shipwreck, the three sailors began to discuss their situation. Dudley, who had been the navigator of the ship, determined that they were at least 1,000 miles from the nearest land and that the storm had blown them far off course from where any ships would normally pass. Stephens, who had been the ship's medical officer, indicated that without food they could not live more than thirty days. The only nourishment they could be assured of was from any rain that might fall from time to time. Stephens noted, however, that if one of the three died before the others, the other two could live awhile longer by eating the body of the third.

On the twenty-fifth day, the third sailor, Brooks, who by this time was extremely weak, suggested that the three of them draw lots and that the loser be killed and eaten by the other two. Both Dudley and Stephens agreed. The next day, lots were drawn and Brooks lost. At this point, Brooks objected and refused to consent. Although Brooks refused to go along, Dudley and Stephens decided that Brooks would die soon anyway, so they might as well get it over with. Brooks was then killed and eaten.

Five days later, Dudley and Stephens were rescued by a passing vessel and brought to port where, after recovering from their ordeal, they were placed on trial for murder.

Problem 2

Assume that international law requires that the law of the home port be applied when a boat is at sea and that the state in which they were tried had the following statute: "Any person who deliberately takes the life of another is guilty of murder."

- **A.** Assume that they are tried for murder and you are on the jury. Would you find them guilty or not guilty? Why?
- **B.** If they are tried and convicted and if you are the judge, what sentence would you impose?
- **C.** Was the boat a separate society? Who made the law there? What similarities do you see between how law was made there and how law is made in a correctional institution?

HOW AND WHERE LAWS ARE MADE

The Constitution

The laws in our country—all of them—must be written and enacted with one law in mind because all other laws must meet its requirements to be valid. That "law" is the Constitution of the United States. It is a remarkable *instrument* in that it was written all at once, with comparatively few drafts, and although it has been added to by way of *amend-*

ment, it has survived today in a society far more complicated than the framers of the Constitution could ever have imagined.

The Constitution is a living, breathing document. The words in it, as interpreted, reflect the current times, conflicts, and changes in society. All laws, in their language, intent, and procedures, must fall within the limits of the Constitution as to what a law may permit or prohibit. For instance, the Constitution requires that laws be written in clear English, that they be unambiguous, and that they not restrict free speech.

As we will see throughout this text, when a law (e.g., a law that restricts free speech) comes into conflict with the Constitution, the highest law in the country, a court is often called on to decide if the law violates the Constitution. Or, for example, if an institution has a policy prohibiting visitors of any race different from that of the inmate, a court may be called upon to decide if this policy violates the Constitution.

Every state also has a constitution or charter that sets out the structure of state government and assigns powers and duties to the various parts of government. The state may also have its own bill of rights that repeats the rights set out in the U.S. Constitution or, sometimes, gives greater rights than those in the U.S. Constitution. More and more inmate lawsuits are filed claiming violations of rights protected under state constitutions. Why are more suits claiming violations of state constitutions? One reason is that recent U.S. Supreme Court interpretations of the U.S. Constitution have narrowed the protections afforded to prisoners.

In many instances, state governments through their state constitutions provide greater protection to individual rights than the federal Constitution. So long as there is no conflict between the federal and state law, states are free to provide greater, but not fewer, rights than the federal Constitution. In fact, from 1970 to 1985, there have been more than 250 appellate opinions that have interpreted rights more broadly under state constitutions than the U.S. Supreme Court has under the federal Constitution.

The drafters of the U.S. Constitution established a government of checks and balances. By separating out the three essential functions of government into three distinct branches—legislative, executive, and judicial—the drafters hoped to avoid the abuse of power.

What are these three essential functions of government? The legislative function sets policy for the future by making predictive value-laden judgments. The executive function implements these policies by making practical, detailed choices how to enforce these policies. The judicial function makes a judgment whether specific behavior violates these policies by evaluating past events.

While each function is assigned to a separate branch of government, the separation is not absolute. In fact, by design, each branch exercises

functions of the other branch. The Presidential pardon is an example of the executive branch exercising a judicial function.

The Legislatures (The Legislative Branch)

Creation   The most familiar lawmaker is the *legislature.* The U.S. Constitution created a Congress consisting of two branches, a House of Representatives and a Senate, and empowered it to pass federal laws. The subjects of these laws include federal crimes, federal taxation, federal courts, U.S. government programs, the national defense, and the national budget. Every U.S. citizen is subject to these federal laws. The constitution or charter of each state establishes the state governing body, which may be called a legislature or general assembly. State legislatures pass laws that apply only in the state. Laws passed by the state and federal legislature are called statutes.

Powers   The U.S. Constitution and state constitutions limit broad legislative power by specifically defining the powers of the legislature. Of importance to correctional personnel are state legislatures' powers to create state agencies, to spend state money, and to establish rights of state employees.

"Enabling statutes" passed by the legislature create the Department of Corrections and other state agencies in most states. The office of sheriff may also be created by the legislature in some states, or it may be created by the state constitution or by county ordinance in others.

Increasing staff and upgrading physical plants and services, improvements that courts have ordered corrections departments to make, can, in the final analysis, only be done by the legislature through appropriation of funds and by laws authorizing and implementing these changes.

Legislators on the federal and state level are having to face greatly reduced abilities to spend money. The legislators represent taxpayers whose priorities generally are not to spend available monies on prisons and jails. This contributes to worsening conditions, more lawsuits, and greater frustration of corrections personnel.

Additionally, determinate sentencing and organized citizen efforts to obtain legislation mandating prison and jail terms for certain offenses have added to the already-existing crisis of overcrowding. Many citizens support locking up offenders and "throwing away the key" while opposing efforts to locate a new facility in their neighborhood or to pay for the resources necessary to *incarcerate* individuals.

Salaries, benefits, and employee rights on the job are mandated by state statutes or by state-sanctioned collective bargaining with public sector employees. State legislatures or their appointed commissions may also pass jail and prison rules and standards; frequently, in this way, the minimum standards for all jails and prisons are set.

Lobbying in the Legislature   Because state legislatures are extensively involved in corrections, it is important for jail and prison personnel to consider when, and in what way, they can bring their concerns to the legislature's attention. Sometimes the views of law enforcement personnel are not heard by lawmakers when legislation is being considered. However, since some states ban *lobbying* by government employees, correctional personnel should investigate what avenues of communication are open to them.

Many Departments of Corrections do have lobbyists working for them. The lobbyists' job is to influence proposed legislation. They do this through personal and written contacts with legislators, through testimony before legislative bodies, and through monitoring bills as they pass through various stages of the legislative process.

The Agencies (The Executive Branch)

Many of the laws that affect corrections personnel are made by government agencies, which make detailed choices on how to implement the policies of the legislature. For example, most state legislatures have passed enabling statutes that set up the state Department of Corrections (a state agency). This department then has the power to make rules governing prisoners and institutions. Disciplinary codes of inmate offenses are examples of agency rules that are usually created by either the Department of Corrections or the local government agency. All agency rules are the law and can only be successfully challenged if the rules go beyond the *scope of authority* given the agency, violate some constitutional rights, or are contrary to some other higher law that applies to that situation.

If the Department of Corrections passed a rule requiring the spouses of all inmates to be employed before being permitted visitor privileges, this rule would go beyond the scope of authority given to the agency by the state legislature. If the department enacted a rule that correctional employees could not belong to a political party, this would violate the U.S. Constitution and possibly the state constitution or state law. Or if the department *enacted* a rule that residents are not entitled to notice of disciplinary offenses before a hearing, this would be contrary to the rule set out by the Supreme Court requiring that inmates be given notice of the offense.

In drawing up regulations for a Department of Corrections or a local jail, administrators must be careful to conform to state laws and the U.S. and state constitutions as written and as they have been interpreted by courts. Failure to do this may result in regulations later being ruled *invalid* in court.

The Courts (The Judicial Branch)

How Courts Make Law   Law is also made by courts. When individuals, businesses, states, associations, and so on have disputes they are unable to resolve, they seek a solution in the courts. The case is brought in a trial court where each party presents its side of the dispute. The jury decides the facts; if there is no jury, the judge decides the facts. The judge interprets and decides the law. This process of interpreting the law is also a process of making law, because whatever the judge says the law is in that case is *binding* on all persons involved.

For example, an inmate sues the jail personnel because the sheriff has a policy that does not permit inmates awaiting trial to attend religious services. An inmate claims this rule has violated his constitutional rights under the First Amendment. The judge must interpret the U.S. Constitution to decide whether *due process* and freedom of religion mean that unconvicted inmates have a right to attend religious services and whether the sheriff must allow ministers to come into the jail to hold services. If the judge finds that the Constitution requires this, the law as it pertains to this jail will be that inmates have a constitutional right to attend religious services.

Except in the most unusual cases, a party may not appeal a decision as to the facts—including the verdict—to an *appellate* court. Issues of fact are decided by trial courts and very rarely are changed by appellate courts. For example, if a trial court found that a jail had been uncom-

fortably cold during the winter (e.g., below fifty-five degrees for thirty days), an appeals court would usually not reverse this decision unless it was obvious from the court record that no evidence had been presented to support that *finding* of fact.

How Courts Are Structured   There are two court systems in every state: state and federal. State courts hear *civil* and *criminal* cases based on state law. Persons charged with violations of state laws are tried in state courts and become state prisoners if convicted. Disputes between citizens of the same state about *contracts* or *injuries* are heard in the civil branch of state trial courts. Federal constitutional questions may also be heard in a state court, although *plaintiffs*—the people bringing the *suit*—generally choose to use federal courts to hear these cases.

There are also appellate courts (both state and federal) to which a losing party may *appeal* from the *verdict* or decision in a trial court. In an appellate court, one party presents written and oral arguments asking the court to change the decision of the trial court, and the other party presents written and oral arguments supporting the decision of the trial court. It is important to remember that appellate courts only hear arguments and make decisions concerning the law involved in the particular case. The judges do not rehear the testimony of witnesses or re-examine all the evidence presented at trial. When a judge makes a decision in a trial as to whether certain evidence may be heard by the jury or when a

---

FIGURE 1 Federal and State Court Systems

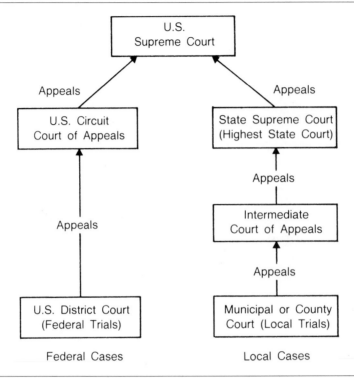

judge instructs the jury, a mistake that may be made will probably be a "legal error." Such legal errors may form the basis of an appeal.

Federal courts hear cases where a federal law or the U.S. Constitution is involved, including civil rights and *habeas corpus* cases. Persons charged with violating federal laws (i.e., federal crimes) are tried in federal courts and become federal prisoners if convicted. Contract and injury cases may also be federal cases where the two parties are from different states and at least $10,000 in damages is claimed.

Throughout the country, federal courts are divided into *circuits*; most circuits include the federal courts in several different states. The ninety-four federal trial courts are called United States District Courts, and the thirteen federal appellate courts are called United States Circuit Courts of Appeals. Note Figure 2 on page 14 to see what circuit your state is in. Because the decisions of your federal circuit court must be followed by all the U.S. District Courts in the states included in your circuit, you should pay particular attention to new decisions involving corrections from your circuit court.

Courts hear both criminal and civil cases. In criminal cases, the government (the state or the United States), represented by the prosecutor, brings charges against the *defendant,* the person accused of committing the crime. If they represent the United States, prosecutors are called Assistant U.S. Attorneys; if they represent the state or local government, they may be called district attorneys, corporation counsel, commonwealth attorneys, county attorneys, or assistant attorneys general. Defense attorneys may be privately hired lawyers. If the defendant cannot afford an attorney, the court may appoint one.

In a civil case, one party (called a plaintiff) sues another (called a defendant), either to collect an amount of money or to force the defendant to do or not do something. There are several different types of civil cases, including actions based on the following sorts of incidents.

- ◆ Joe is injured by Derek when Derek rearends Joe's car. Joe sues Derek to pay his medical bills, to repair his car, and to pay for pain and suffering incurred.

- ◆ Mr. Garfield, a landlord, wants Gerry to leave his apartment. He sues Gerry for possession of the apartment (eviction).

- ◆ Inmate Franklin falls down the steps at the jail on his way to lunch and breaks his leg. He claims another inmate pushed him and that the correctional officer saw it and made no effort to stop the other inmate or to assist Franklin once he had fallen. He sues the officer for damages.

- ◆ Jones is fired from the Department of Corrections. He claims discrimination and files suit asking that the department be ordered to reinstate him and give him back pay.

Most of the problems discussed in this book will be civil cases. Typical examples will be situations where inmates are injured and file suit in a state or federal court for damages.

There are a number of specialized branches of trial courts, usually at the county or city level, which hear only certain types of cases. Examples of such courts are Small Claims Court (cases involving very small amounts of money), Landlord-Tenant Court (cases involving disputes between landlords and tenants), Family or Domestic Relations Court (cases involving divorce, separation, custody of children), and Civil Court (cases involving larger amounts of money).

As you can see on the court system diagram (Figure 1, page 12), trials can be held in either the U.S. District Court (for a federal case) or the local state court (may be called a county, district, or circuit court). If you lose your case (trial) in the U.S. District Court, you can appeal to a U.S. Court of Appeals and, if you lose again, to the U.S. Supreme Court. (Actually, the U.S. Supreme Court agrees to hear less than two percent

FIGURE 2 The Thirteen Federal Judicial Circuits

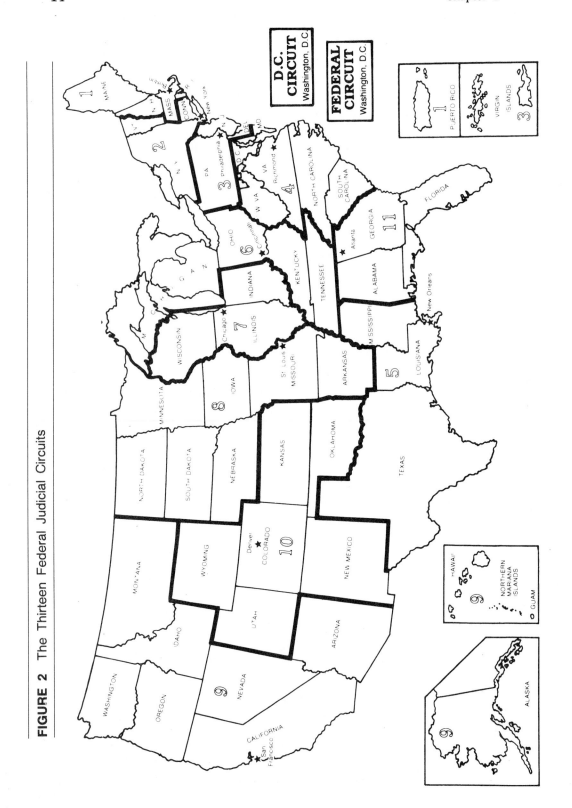

of the cases it is asked to decide.) If you lose your case (trial) in your local trial court, you can usually appeal either directly to the State Supreme Court or first to an intermediate court of appeals, if your state has one, and then to the state's highest court. Sometimes State Supreme Court decisions can be appealed to the U.S. Supreme Court.

Let us suppose that, in a certain case, the U.S. Court of Appeals decides two to one (majority rule) to reverse the decision of the trial court. Usually the Court of Appeals will issue a written opinion stating why it *ruled* as it did. This opinion is called a *precedent,* which means that in the future all judges in lower courts in the place (circuit) where the decision was made must follow the rule (or law) in the case. This is what we mean by courts making law. In the future, other courts may interpret the opinion of the U.S. Court of Appeals and attempt to apply the general reasoning of the Court of Appeals in similar fact situations. You should note that a higher court—or the same court, if another case comes before it—can *reverse* this precedent and issue a new precedent. This might happen if judges die or retire and new judges come to the court or if the judges change their minds. The most important precedents are set in cases heard and decided by the U.S. Supreme Court in Washington, D.C. (Nine judges hear each case, and the majority determines the outcome.) All courts in the United States must follow U.S. Supreme Court decisions.

Precedents are very important to our whole system of law. Not only must other courts follow the law announced in these cases but the written decisions are incorporated in the law books that lawyers use to prepare written and oral arguments for their cases in court.

Sometimes the term "precedent" is used in a general sense to refer to the same or similar cases decided in other states or other federal circuits. Though no court is required to follow these kinds of "precedents," a court may choose to do so, because it finds the reasoning used persuasive.

 ### The Case of Johnson v. Avery

An inmate challenged a Tennessee State Penitentiary rule that prohibited inmates from assisting other inmates in preparing writs "or other legal matters." In fact, the inmate had been punished for violating the rule. A writ of habeas corpus was filed in the U.S. District Court where the penitentiary was located. After a hearing, that court held that the regulation in question was void because it prevented prisoners who could not read or write from access to federal courts. The U.S. Court of Appeals (Sixth Circuit), which takes Tennessee appeals, reversed and ruled against the inmate, stating that the state had a legitimate interest in limiting the practice of law to licensed attorneys.

Such limitations had always been the *rule* as established by a number of prior cases in Tennessee and many other states; that is, the state could limit the practice of law to licensed attorneys and could prohibit inmates from assisting other inmates in legal matters.

However, after an appeal to the U.S. Supreme Court, the rule, or "precedent," was changed. The Supreme Court held that, unless the state provides reasonable alternatives to assist inmates in the preparation of petitions for post-conviction relief, the state must allow inmates to furnish legal assistance to other prisoners.

Thus, the precedent was changed; that is, whereas the state had previously been permitted to prevent one inmate from providing legal assistance to another inmate, the state would now either have to provide reasonable alternatives for such help or permit one inmate to assist another. Because this new precedent was set by the U.S. Supreme Court, it applied to every jail and prison in the United States.[1]

When court decisions establish precedents, they decide the issues in the case before them and sometimes also state a general rule that will have to be interpreted in future cases.

Appellate courts do not decide every issue that may later arise. Thus, after the *Johnson v. Avery* case just described, future cases would have to decide what would be a "reasonable alternative" to allowing inmates to act as jailhouse lawyers, as well as other issues related to this, such as access to law libraries, the right to an appointed attorney, and the right to write letters to attorneys, courts, and other legal organizations.

The Corporal Punishment Case History

In 1965, inmates in the Arkansas State Prison filed suit claiming that, because they broke prison rules, they had been whipped with a five-foot-long, four-inch-wide, quarter-inch-thick strap by assistant wardens and an inmate trusty. They claimed this *corporal punishment* violated the Eighth Amendment to the U.S. Constitution, which prohibits "cruel and unusual punishment."

The U.S. District Court ruled against the inmates, finding that corporal punishment was a method of enforcing discipline that had been used for many years in Arkansas and other states. The District Court also found that, although the U.S. Supreme Court had not ruled on the issue, the Supreme Courts of Delaware and Florida had upheld the practice. The court did order that rules be developed listing what offenses could be punished and how much whipping could be received for each.[2]

In 1967, other inmates filed suit, again claiming that corporal punishment and use of the strap were cruel and unusual punishment, but the court again denied the inmates' claims. The court relied on the 1965 decision and on the historical viewpoint that accepted corporal punishment and the strap as a permissible form of punishment.[3] This time, the inmates appealed to the U.S. Court of Appeals (8th Circuit), which in 1968 reversed the District Court decision and ruled for the inmates, stating that use of a strap and corporal punishment offend concepts of decency and human dignity that have existed in the 20th century.[4] The Court of Appeals did not cite specific case precedents but said that corporal punishment made inmates "hate" prison personnel, that it frustrated goals of corrections, and that public opinion was against it.

Problem 3

A. What were the three court decisions in the preceding case history?

First Two against inmates, U.S. District Court

Last one For inmates - U.S. Court of appeals

B. Upon what did the District Court base its decision in the 1965 case? Was the 1965 decision binding on any prisons? *Used for years in arkansas + other states*

C. Upon what did the District Court base its 1967 decision? Did it have to rule as it did, or could it have decided differently?

D. Upon what did the Court of Appeals base its 1968 decision? Didn't this court have to follow the other precedents mentioned in the case history? Explain.

E. Does the 1968 decision mean that correctional officers cannot use force against inmates under any circumstances?

F. Because the U.S. Supreme Court still has not ruled in a case involving corporal punishment in prisons, could a state prison use a strap to punish inmates?

THE COURT'S ROLE IN CORRECTIONAL ADMINISTRATION

In recent years, the issues of how much power the courts have, should have, or should extend over correctional institutions have frequently been raised. Prior to the 1960s, the courts were reluctant to interfere with the day-to-day operation of prisons and jails. Early federal court decisions frequently expressed the general policy of leaving prison and jail administration solely to correctional officials. But the social and legal revolutions of the 1960s altered this "hands-off" policy. A "hands-on" attitude dominated the 1960s and 1970s, when numerous lawsuits were filed seeking the identification and protection of prisoner rights.

In 1979, the U.S. Supreme Court under Chief Justice Warren Burger signaled a change in the approach of court intervention in correctional administration. Dubbed by some the "one-hand-on, one-hand-off" approach, it encouraged federal judges to identify the existence of constitutional rights' violations but to defer to the expertise of jail and prison officials in the administration of the institution. Only when the officials fail to correct an identified violation should federal courts issue detailed orders on how to correct such a violation.

Note the words of Chief Justice William Rehnquist in the Supreme Court case of *Bell v. Wolfish:*

> The deplorable conditions and draconian restrictions of some of our nation's prisons are too well known to require recounting here, and the federal courts rightly have condemned these sordid aspects of our prison systems. But many of these same courts have, in the name of the Constitution, become increasingly enmeshed in the minutiae of prison operations. Judges, after all, are human. They, no less than others in our society, have a natural tendency

to believe that their individual solutions to often intractable problems are better and more workable than those of the persons who are actually charged with and trained in the running of the particular institution under examination.[5]

Problem 4

The city of Ecalpon operates a jail that was constructed many years ago. After fifty-one years of continuous use, the jail facilities are in disrepair, the furnace does not adequately heat the building, the electrical system poses a potential fire hazard, and rotting and falling plaster and wood have resulted in many injuries to officers and inmates. All manner of rats, mice, and some unrecognizable rodents and insects also inhabit the jail. The fire marshal has condemned the building, the Housing Department has issued thousands of citations against the jail, and the Health Department has ordered the facility closed. Of course, nothing has been done because all these departments, like the local jail itself, are part of the city of Ecalpon. The mayor has stated that the situation is deplorable, but there is nothing he can do because the City Council refuses to set aside funds to make the necessary repairs. Four inmates bring suit to require the city to repair its jail or, as an alternative, close the building.

    A. Is the suit filed by the inmates a civil or criminal suit?

    B. Would the inmates bring the suit in federal court or in state court?

    C. List several laws or regulations involved in the case. Are they constitutional, federal, state, or local?

    D. Do court precedents have any bearing on what the court does in this case?

    E. List possible results in this case. If you were the judge, what would you do in this case?

    F. Will agencies or legislatures be involved in this case after it is decided? Explain.

CORRECTIONAL STANDARDS

In recent years, many organizations have undertaken the development of correctional and jail standards. The American Correctional Association has created a commission comprised of correctional and criminal justice administrators. The commission has developed standards for

both adult jails and prisons, as well as a system of accreditation whereby an institution may provide funds to pay for an inspection. Following inspection, the institution, if it is found to comply with a certain percentage of the standards, receives a certificate of accreditation. Other organizations that have drafted correctional and jail standards include the American Bar Association, the U.S. Department of Justice, the United Nations, the National Sheriffs' Association, the American Medical Association, and the American Public Health Association. Unfortunately, the standards adopted by different organizations differ, and much controversy exists over which standards should be followed.

The reasons institutions or departments of corrections adopt standards or try to comply with certain standards include the following:

- ◆ to prevent problems from occurring in the institutions that may result in *lawsuits;*
- ◆ to use compliance with the standards as a basis for defense in a lawsuit;
- ◆ to settle a lawsuit;
- ◆ as the basis of a court order; and
- ◆ to evaluate correctional programs and to use the results as the basis for financial requests from the federal and state and local governments.

It should be noted that, unless a governmental body formally adopts standards or a court orders them, compliance is voluntary. In other words, standards do not become legally binding until they have been adopted by a state legislature, a court decision or promulgated as regulations. There is controversy over whether the federal government should adopt mandatory standards for either federal or state institutions. Many courts look at the different standards when deciding cases and may even select a particular standard as the basis for deciding whether rights of inmates have been violated.

Problem 5

A. Which of the following groups of people should be involved in writing or passing standards? Why?

1. Inmates
2. Lawyers
3. Sheriffs
4. Correctional administrators
5. Correctional officers
6. State legislators
7. Members of Congress
8. Federal officials
9. Judges
10. Citizens in the community

B. Should there be mandatory or advisory standards issued by the federal government? Explain.

C. Should judges use standards in making decisions in corrections cases? Why?

LEGAL RESEARCH

Throughout this book, references or citations ("cites") are made to various cases and laws relevant to corrections. This section is included to help you understand what these cites mean and how to find the law. Some readers will wish to understand a case, law, or regulation better by reading it.

The law as it is written by judges in opinions, by agencies in rules, and by legislatures in statutes is contained in many volumes in law

libraries. The ability to find the law on a particular subject in these
volumes is a valuable and useful skill to acquire. Some corrections
departments have set up law libraries for their employees so that correctional personnel may read the laws that set out their rights and duties.
Other institutions have libraries principally for inmates, but correctional personnel can also use them.

Statutes and Regulations

Laws made by legislatures are called statutes or codes. Laws passed by
every state legislature are contained in state codes, and those enacted by
Congress are contained in the U.S. Code. Statutes passed in one state do
not apply in other states, while statutes passed by Congress are binding on
all citizens.

In order to find the statutes, you must first locate the proper code. For
example, the Civil Rights Attorney Fees Award Act of 1976 is cited as
42 U.S.C. § 1988. The federal code is indicated by U.S.C., which stands
for United States Code. The title number of the code is 42, and 1988 is
the section. Therefore, you locate the volume of the U.S. Code with a 42
on the outside and then locate the page(s) with § 1988.

Regulations made by agencies are located in registers or codes. For
example, regulations made by federal agencies are printed in the *Code of
Federal Regulations* and the *Federal Register*. The *Code of Federal Regulations*
contains fifty titles representing broad areas subject to federal regula-

tion. Each title contains chapters bearing the name of the federal agency issuing the regulation. Each chapter contains parts representing specific regulatory areas. This code has a subject index to help locate the regulations. To keep readers apprised of recent amendments and revisions to federal regulations, the *Federal Register,* published daily, provides lists of parts and sections changed and the changes themselves.

Case Law

Laws are made by judges who interpret statutes and decide cases that come before them. These judicial (or court) decisions are contained in volumes called reports or reporters. Since there are state, federal, and often local court systems, it is necessary to keep in mind which court decisions are binding upon which courts. A state's highest appeals court decisions will be precedent for all the state's future lower court (appellate and trial) decisions. In the federal court system, the higher court (that is, the U.S. Court of Appeals) will bind the lower courts (that is, the U.S. District Courts). U.S. Supreme Court decisions are precedent for all courts in the country.

References to cases first give the case name and then its cite and the date of the decision. Examples:

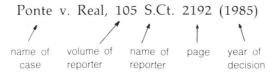

The reporters are organized according to which court has issued the opinion. As new cases are decided by courts, the opinions are published in pamphlet form and are called advance sheets. Later these advance sheets are bound together in the proper reporter's most recent volume.

U.S. Supreme Court   Decisions of the U.S. Supreme Court, the highest federal court, are found in several reporters: *United States Reports,* cited "U.S."; in *Supreme Court Reporter,* cited "S.Ct."; and in *Lawyer's Edition,* cited "L.Ed." Examples:

465 U.S. 870 (1984)
104 S.Ct. 152 (1984)
79 L.Ed.2d 878 (1984)

The most recent Supreme Court opinions are found in weekly editions of the *United States Law Weekly* (U.S.L.W.), a multi-volume set of loose leafs. Example:

U.S. Court of Appeals   Decisions of these federal appeals courts from the 13 circuits (see diagram on p. 14) are found in the *Federal Reporter,* cited "F." for the first series containing older decisions and "F.2d" for the second series containing more recent decisions. Example:

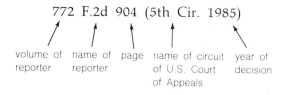

U.S. District Court   Decisions of the U.S. District Courts are found in the *Federal Supplement,* cited "F.Supp." Examples:

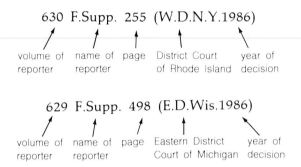

State Courts of Appeal   The states are organized into several regions. The highest court decisions are found in the regional reporter covering that particular state. These reporters include: *Pacific Reporter,* cited "P."; *Atlantic Reporter,* cited "A."; *South Western Reporter,* cited "S.W."; *South Eastern Reporter,* cited "S.E."; and *Southern Reporter,* cited "So." More recent decisions are in the second series (2d) of the reporter. Example:

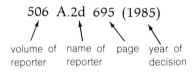

506 A.2d 695 (1985)

volume of   name of   page   year of
reporter   reporter   decision

Many states have their own reporter systems that contain opinions issued by the state's courts. Example:

221 Cal.Rptr. 146 (1985)

volume of   name of   page   year of
reporter   reporter   decision

Shepardizing

Shepard's Citations is a publication that reports on the present status of all cases and statutes—that is, whether the law has been overruled, cited, followed in other states, and so on. Before ever stating that a case is the latest on a particular topic, that case should be "Shepardized" to make sure the law has not been changed.

Research Techniques

There is no way in this introductory chapter to teach legal research in any depth. Readers who wish to develop their legal-research skills more fully are advised to refer to *West's Law Finder* (West Publishing Company, St. Paul, MN).

References

1. Johnson v. Avery, 393 U.S. 483, 89 S.Ct. 747 (1969).
2. Talley v. Stephens, 247 F.Supp. 683 (E.D.Ark.1965).
3. Jackson v. Bishop, 268 F.Supp. 804 (E.D.Ark.1967).
4. Jackson v. Bishop, 404 F.2d 571 (8th Cir.1968).
5. 441 U.S. 520, 99 S.Ct. 1861 (1979).

CHAPTER 2

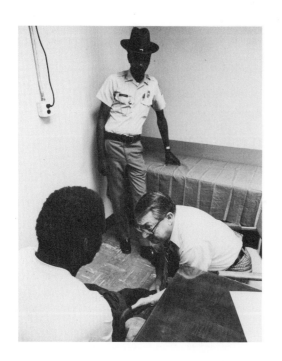

Rights and Liabilities of Jail and Prison Personnel

THE RIGHT TO USE FORCE

Generally, society does not allow one person to use force against another, and, under some circumstances, even a verbal threat may constitute a crime. Use of force against another constitutes the crime of *assault* and may result in a civil lawsuit whereby the person assaulted may sue the attacker for any damages caused. There are, however, certain circumstances in which law enforcement officers may use force and when it is their duty or "right" to do so. In the circumstances where force is permitted, law enforcement officers may be guilty of criminal assault if excessive force is used and may be liable for money damages from a civil lawsuit in which the arrested or assaulted person (or inmate) sues the officer.

In the following section, the law of the use of force will be discussed. Be aware, however, that the law in your state may be somewhat different from this necessarily general discussion. The law in the state where the institution is located is the standard by which the courts will determine whether the exercise of force was proper. Generally, there are four circumstances in which a correctional officer has the right to use force:

1. self-defense;
2. defending or aiding another (officer, inmate, or visitor);
3. enforcing institutional regulations; and
4. preventing the commission of a crime, including escape.

27

It is difficult to state exactly how much force may be used in each of these situations, though the general rule is that the amount of force must be reasonable and necessary under the circumstances. The standard for reasonableness is that of the reasonable and prudent correctional officer. What would such an objective officer do under the circumstances? If the case goes to court, this is what the judge or jury (if a jury trial) must decide.

Nondeadly Force

The most common situation in which correctional personnel have a right to use force is when they are assaulted by an inmate or inmates. In general, personnel may use such reasonable force as may be, or reasonably appears to be, necessary to protect themselves, but they should only use the amount of force required to subdue the inmate. This is called self-defense.

Correctional personnel also have a right to use force to help another correctional officer, an inmate, or anyone under attack. Again, in these situations, the personnel may use such reasonable force as may be, or reasonably appears to be, necessary to protect anyone but should only use the amount of force required to subdue the attacker. If the officer continues to use force after stopping the attacker, the roles reverse, and the defender becomes the attacker and the one committing the assault.

Here are some examples of recent cases that illustrate how the courts try to handle nondeadly force situations.

1. After a riot was subdued in a state prison, an attempt was made to segregate inmates who had participated. As one inmate was being taken to a maximum security cell, he was beaten with clubs by two prison officers. The court found this use of force to be unreasonable and awarded a $3,000 judgment against the two prison officers and the captain of the officer force.[1]

2. A fight occurred between five inmates and a number of officers. The inmates suffered severe cuts, broken bones, and other injuries. One officer was hurt so badly he was taken to intensive care. After hearing the evidence, the court found that the inmates were resisting prison authority and that the force used to subdue them was reasonable and necessary.[2]

Traditionally, force also could be used to enforce institutional regulations, but this often resulted in what many people felt was unnecessary corporal punishment. Modern correctional philosophy calls for personnel to use force only as a last resort to enforce regulations and, even then, to use only the minimum amount required. In describing its model rule on the use of force to enforce institutional regulations, the American Correctional Association Law Project states: "While the model allows physical methods to enforce institutional regulations, it is hoped that the trend toward less physical control of inmates will be undertaken. Control and management of offenders should be by sound scientific

methods, stressing moral values and organized persuasion, rather than primary dependence upon physical force." [3]

Therefore, to grab or strike an inmate who is talking out of turn or walking out of line could give rise to liability if the officer did not first attempt to correct the situation through a verbal reprimand. On the other hand, an inmate who is found writing on the wall in a jail dormitory and continues to do so after an officer tells him to stop can be physically moved away from the wall. Again, the standard will be whether what the officer did under the circumstances was "reasonable."

Another difficult issue concerns the type of force correctional personnel may use. For example, when can correctional personnel use mechanical restraints, chemical agents, tear gas, and so on? Clearly, such devices can be an effective and necessary means of maintaining order, especially in particularly dangerous situations, such as riots or other types of prison disturbances. But some believe that such devices should not be used unless absolutely necessary.

Mechanical restraints are most commonly used to prevent escape when transporting inmates or to protect inmates whose past history and

---

**Correctional Law Project's
(American Correctional Association)
Model Correctional Rules and Regulations***

II. Non-Deadly Force

  A. Non-deadly force is force which normally causes neither death nor serious bodily injury. It may be in the form of physical force or chemical agents.

    1. Physical force or chemical agents may be used only in the following instances:

      a. Prior to the use of deadly force

        1. To prevent the commission of a *felony,* including escape.

        2. To prevent an act which could result in death or severe bodily harm to one's self or to another person.

      b. In defending one's self or others against any physical assault.

      c. To prevent commission of a *misdemeanor.*

      d. To prevent serious damage to property.

      e. To enforce institutional regulations.

      f. To prevent or *quell* a riot.

In every case, only the minimum force necessary shall be used.

    2. Chemical Agents—Special Conditions

      a. Chemical agents may be used only by employees specifically trained in their use.

      b. Chemical agents shall not be used:

        1. Without approval of the warden or his representative, if approval is possible under the circumstances.

        2. Repeatedly against an inmate within a short period of time.

      c. In every case, individuals affected by the agents shall be permitted to wash their face, eyes or other exposed skin areas as soon as possible after the use of the agent.

B. After the use of non-deadly force, the following steps shall be undertaken:
  1. A notification of its use shall be given to the warden.
  2. A report written by the officer who employed the non-deadly force shall be filed with the Director of the Department of Corrections. Such report shall include:
    a. An accounting of the events leading to the use of the non-deadly force.
    b. A precise description of the incident, and the reasons for employing the force.
    c. A description of the weapon used, if any, and the manner in which it was used.
    d. A description of the injuries suffered, if any, and the treatment given.
    e. A list of all participants and witnesses to the incident.
C. The use of any type of force for punishment or reprisal is strictly prohibited and is *grounds* for dismissal of the employee involved.

III. Mechanical Restraints
  A. Mechanical restraints may be used only when reasonably necessary and only in the following instances:
    1. In transporting an inmate from place to place.
    2. When the past history and present behavior or apparent emotional state of the inmate creates the likelihood that bodily injury to any person or escape by the inmate will occur.
    3. Under medical advice, to prevent the inmate from attempting suicide or inflicting serious physical injury upon himself.
  B. Mechanical restraints shall never be used:
    1. As a method of punishment.
    2. About the head or neck of the inmate.
    3. In a way that causes undue physical discomfort, inflicts physical pain or restricts the blood circulation or breathing of the inmate.

---

* See Appendix D.

present behavior create the likelihood that they will injure themselves or others. Liability can result in situations where such restraints are used as punishment or when they are applied about the head or neck of an inmate in a manner that causes *undue* physical discomfort, inflicts physical pain, or restricts the inmate's blood circulation or breathing.

Chemical agents should be used only by those trained to use them, and injuries resulting from improper use, especially by someone who is untrained, may result in liability for individual officers, their supervisors, the institution, or the department as a whole. Failure to follow institutional rules regarding the use of these agents, such as the requirement of first receiving the warden's permission, may also result in liability.

One court has held that the use of mace, tear gas, or other chemical agents was appropriate to prevent riots or escape or subdue disobeying inmates in a major segregation unit of a maximum security prison. It did not violate the Constitution, even if the inmates are locked in their prison cells or are in handcuffs, because it was viewed by the court as "reasonably necessary." [4]

In another case, a federal court found prison officials liable when they failed to take preventative action in response to incidents in which correctional officers routinely used high-pressure hoses against securely confined inmates. An inmate locked in his cell was sprayed with high-pressure hoses, maced, and beaten with clubs by the officers. [5]

The evidence presented in a given case is extremely important. For example, in one case, an inmate claimed that officers beat him up, broke his nose, rammed his head into a grate, and sprayed him with mace for no reason. The court ruled against the inmate when he presented four witnesses, all of whom disagreed with one another and gave different accounts of what had happened.

A key question that judges or juries often ask themselves in deciding if excessive force was used is "Were the officers using force because it was necessary to subdue the inmate, or were they using it for purposes of punishment?" The courts have made it clear that corporal punishment may not be used against inmates and that correctional institutions must find other methods of disciplining prisoners. In addition, some states have laws (and most Departments of Corrections have rules) prohibiting such conduct. It should be remembered that when correctional employees violate the law or their own rules, this may form the basis of a civil lawsuit against them or subject them to disciplinary action within their agency.

Problem 6

Using the Model Rules and Regulations set out on the preceding pages, determine in each case whether the correctional personnel had a right to use the force employed and, if not, what the officer should have done.

A. Officer Lewis is assigned to the jail intake unit. Three inmates are present and handcuffed. Lewis indicates in a somewhat abusive manner to Inmate Frank that he is to strip down for the customary intake search. He unhandcuffs Frank and, in response to the instruction, Frank swings around and hits Lewis squarely on the jaw. Lewis, dazed, responds by slugging Frank, knocking him down, and then handcuffing him to restrain him.

Was Frank coming at him?

B. Inmate Simmons refused to enter a punishment cell, having just received a negative decision from the Adjustment Board. Officer Jones, accompanying Simmons, tells him to go into the cell, whereupon Simmons responds by yelling, "Shove it!" Jones pushes Simmons into the cell with such force that the inmate smashes into the wall ten feet away. *HAD Right*

C. Officer Marshall discovers that Inmate Smith has violated institutional rules by sneaking food out of the dining room back to his cell. Smith yells an obscenity at Marshall. Marshall slaps Smith. *No Right*

D. Inmate Green went on a rampage, setting mattresses on fire and wrecking his cell. He was transferred to an isolation cell where he requested medical and psychiatric care. He was told he would be required to wait. He again set his mattress on fire. A correctional officer tear gassed him and left him alone in the cell for eleven hours. *Abusive - No Right - Restrain him*

E. Inmate Ferrari was continually yelling from his cell at officers and other inmates to protest the poor conditions in the jail. He was warned repeatedly to stop his disruptive behavior but continued to act this way. Officer Moore and his supervisor, Captain Friendly, tear gassed Ferrari's cell. *- No Right - Isolate him*

Deadly Force

The *general* rule is that deadly force can be used in only two instances:

1. To prevent a felony, sometimes including escape; and
2. To prevent an act that could result in death or severe bodily injury.

It is well established that deadly force can be used only as a last resort. If used at any other time, such force may result in civil and/or criminal liability against the user. The general rules regarding self-defense also apply in that persons defending themselves or others may use only that amount of force reasonably necessary to subdue the attacker.

The question of whether deadly force should be used to stop a prison or jail escape is a difficult one. In most states, an escape is a felony; therefore, many people argue that, in those states, deadly force always can be used to stop an escape. Others say that deadly force can only be used against a person known to be "dangerous." Others disagree and argue that fleeing convicted *felons* can be stopped through the use of deadly force. If this is the law, another problem may arise in an institution where both felons and *misdemeanants* are lodged. Is it the responsibility of the officer in the tower of a prison to determine if the escaping inmate is a felon or a misdemeanant before using deadly force? Should it make a difference if the inmate has been convicted or is being held

---

Correctional Law Projects
(American Correctional Association)
Model Correctional Rules and Regulations*

I. Deadly Force

   A. Deadly force is force which will likely cause death or serious bodily injury.

   B. It may be used only as a last resort and then only in the following instances:

      1. To prevent the commission of a felony, including escape.

      2. To prevent an act which could result in death or severe bodily injury to one's self or to another person.

   C. When used, the following steps shall be undertaken:

      1. An immediate notification of its use shall be given to the warden and to the proper law enforcement authorities.

      2. A report written by the officer who used the deadly force shall be filed with the Director of the Department of Corrections, and the proper law enforcement authorities. Such report shall include:

         a. An accounting of the events leading to the use of deadly force.

         b. A precise description of the incident and the reasons for employing the deadly force.

         c. A description of the weapon and the manner in which it was used.

         d. A description of the injuries suffered, if any, and the treatment given.

         e. A list of all participants and witnesses to the incident.

---

* See Appendix D.

---

before trial in a jail? These questions have not always been answered by the courts.

In a 1985 case, *Tennessee v. Garner,* the U.S. Supreme Court held that police cannot use deadly force in escape situations unless: (1) it is necessary to prevent the escape and (2) the officer has probable cause to believe that the suspect poses a significant threat of death or serious physical injury to the officer or others.[6] At least one state Department of Corrections has interpreted this ruling to apply to escapes from prisons. Under this interpretation, deadly force cannot be used to prevent escapes from prison unless deadly force is necessary and the officer has probable cause to believe that the escaping inmate poses a significant threat of death or serious physical injury to the officer or others. Later cases may clarify this situation.

To determine what should be done when a prisoner attempts an escape, you should carefully check the law in each state by examining the state statutes, court cases, and regulations of the Departments of Corrections and/or correctional institutions.

In 1986, the U.S. Supreme Court in a five-four decision clarified the circumstances under which the use of force to quell a prison disturbance amounts to a violation of the Constitution.[7] Prison officials, in this case, were attempting to release an officer taken hostage who was held in a second tier cell. The prison security manager's plan called for the security manager to enter the cellblock unarmed followed by officers armed with shotguns. The security manager ordered one officer to fire a warning shot and to shoot low any inmate climbing the stairs to the upper tier. Inmate Albers, after attempting to help elderly inmates avoid tear gassing, decided to return to his own cell on the second tier for safety. One officer fired a warning shot and then shot this inmate in the knee.

The inmate filed a lawsuit claiming this use of force was cruel and unusual punishment. The Supreme Court disagreed. The test whether the prison security measure undertaken to restore a disturbance violates the Constitution is whether the force was applied in a good-faith effort to maintain or restore discipline or maliciously and sadistically for the very purpose of causing harm.

The Court identified these factors as being relevant: (1) the need for the application of force, (2) the relationship between the need and the amount of force used, (3) the extent of the injury inflicted, (4) the extent of threat to safety of staff and inmates as reasonably perceived by the responsible officer on the basis of facts known to them, and (5) any effort made to temper the severity of a forceful response.

The inmate may have a valid _tort_ claim for battery in this case, but his constitutional rights were not violated.[8]

Another potential area of liability if deadly force is used lies with supervisory personnel and the department as a whole, both for failing to provide adequate training in the use of firearms, for entrusting a weapon to someone whom supervisors knew or reasonably should have known was incompetent to use it, and for failing to instruct when such force may be used. Some states have laws or rules requiring such training, and failure to provide required training may impose grounds for liability on additional persons. For example, in 1985, a court of appeals ordered the sheriff to pay $125,000 for failure to train and discipline his officers. The court had found that the sheriff had approved the use of wanton brutality by members of his force.[9]

Problem 7

Officer Burke, assigned to a guard tower about 100 feet from the gate, opens the gate to allow Officer Bradley to enter along with an inmate returning from court. Burke observes the inmate, who is handcuffed, reach down to pull something out of his left shoe. Bradley's back is turned, he is five feet in front of the inmate, and he is unarmed. Officer Burke has a shotgun in the tower.

    A. How much, if any, force is he allowed to use to protect Bradley from the possible attack by the inmate? What should Burke do?

Yell to Officer Bradley - Tell inmate to Freeze

    B. What if Burke saw the inmate pull a shiny object out of his shoe? Do you agree or disagree with the statement, "Officer Burke should fire his weapon at the inmate"?

Yell to inmate to put down weapon or be shot

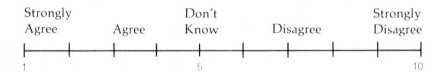

Strongly Agree	Agree	Don't Know	Disagree	Strongly Disagree
1		5		10

    C. What if Burke is certain the shiny object was a knife? Does your opinion change? *Yes - Shoot to wound.*

Problem 8

Correctional Officer Murray works at a state prison where both felons and misdemeanants are housed. He observes an inmate climbing the wall from the recreation yard that leads to a wide space and then to a twelve-foot fence with barbed wire on the top. The officer has a shotgun. What should the officer do? In his state, escape by a felon is a felony, and the state law only allows the use of deadly force against fleeing felons. Would your answer be different if your state courts had held that the *Tennessee v. Garner* decision applied to prison escapes?

Yell, Stop or I'll shoot - then fire a warning shot if necessary - should not have to shoot prisoner. Will have time to apprehend.

Problem 9

Inmates in a state prison have taken three officers hostage and refuse to release them until a helicopter is provided for their escape. Prison officials refuse their demand. Can correctional officers use deadly force to try to secure the release of the officers? *Only if Officers lives are threatened?*

Problem 10

Officer Wilson sees an inmate running for the wall of the prison yard. He fires but misses and hits another inmate, who is watching but not trying to escape. Officer Wilson has never received training in the proper use of firearms. If the wounded inmate sues, who may be liable for damages? *Institution*

SITUATIONS INVOLVING POSSIBLE LIABILITY OF JAIL AND PRISON PERSONNEL

Recently, more cases have been filed against correctional personnel by inmates who have been injured, by the families of inmates who have died while incarcerated, or by other persons who have been injured by inmates where some fault on the part of correctional personnel is claimed.

Vicarious Liability

In situations where an inmate dies or is injured, the officer actually carrying out the act may be liable for the injuries. It is possible and even probable that others may be liable as well—others who may not even have been physically present when the incident took place. This is called vicarious liability. When applied to the employer-employee relationship, it is called "respondeat superior," which means "let the superior answer." The result is that the employer may be responsible for the torts (wrongful acts) of employees, if the acts were committed while the employees were engaged in activity falling within the scope of their employment.

The underlying rationale for the employer's vicarious liability is to find a financially responsible defendant to pay for the injuries caused the plaintiff. Courts have stated that, since an employer has control over the employees—having selected, hired, assigned, and supervised them—he or she is also the proper person, in addition to the employees themselves, to hold liable for their acts. Who is held liable is the top officials and/or the unit of government involved. For example, when an escaped inmate raped four women, the city of the District of Columbia was held vicariously liable and ordered to pay $180,000.[10]

However, in Section 1983 civil rights lawsuits, respondeat superior does not apply. The agency or employer is not automatically liable for constitutional violations committed by its employees. Instead, they are liable for constitutional violations committed by subordinates only where they have established a governmental policy or custom that is affirmatively linked to the subordinate's violation of constitutional rights.

For example, if the supervisor in charge of classification is aware that subordinates routinely classify Hispanics in a high-security status simply because they are Hispanic and if he or she takes no corrective action, the supervisor has established a custom that may subject him or her to liability for the actions of the staff.

There are at least four ways the required affirmative link can be established between the custom or policy and the subordinate's violation of constitutional rights. One, the supervisor personally participated; for example, the supervisor directed the employee to act or the employee acted with the knowledge and consent of the supervisor. Two, the supervisor breaches a duty imposed by state or local law, by action or inaction. Three, the supervisor knew or should have known of the employee's misconduct and fails to prevent it from happening again. And, four, the supervisor acquiesces by inaction (goes along with) after learning about the injuries caused by the subordinate.

In *Oklahoma City v. Tuttle,* the Supreme Court ruled that one incident of excessive force does not amount to a policy or custom necessary to impose liability on the unit of local government.[11] In a plurality opinion, the Court stated that proof of a single incident of unconstitutional employee activity is not enough to hold a municipality liable unless there is proof that the incident was caused by an existing unconstitutional policy that can be attributed to a municipal policymaker. Otherwise, the Court said, the existence of the unconstitutional policy and its origin must be separately proved.

The Supreme Court also said that, where the policy itself is not unconstitutional, considerably more proof than a single incident will be necessary in every case to establish both the fault on the part of the municipality and the causal connection between the policy and the constitutional violation.[12]

In 1986, the Supreme Court ruled that municipal liability may be imposed for a single decision by municipal policymakers under certain situations. If the decision to adopt a particular course of action is directed by those who establish governmental policy, the municipality is responsible, whether that action is to be taken only once or several times.[13]

Supervisors of negligent employees may also be held liable for the actions of their officers on the theory of vicarious liability. For supervisors to be liable, they must have failed to direct or train their officers or must have been negligent in hiring, supervising, assigning, or retaining them. The supervisor's failure or negligence must have contributed to the *negligence* of the officer. This is different from respondeat superior, which places liability on the employer without a finding of fault.

For instance, if the captain fails to provide weapons training and then assigns to the tower an untrained officer who shoots and harms an innocent inmate, the captain may be liable for the inmate's injuries. The government unit (the state, for instance) may be automatically liable for the captain's negligence and the officer's negligence.

The existence of a written manual of operating policies and procedures that actually is used as a guide and is kept up-to-date may be a valid defense to a claim that supervisors failed to direct. Supervisors should also train all personnel in departmental policies and procedures, and such training should be documented.

To prove negligence in hiring, supervising, assigning, or retaining an officer, the injured person must show that the supervisor knew or should have known of the employee's past conduct or habits that were evidence of the employee's potential for negligent conduct.

Problem 11 ♦ *Supervisory Liability: Case Studies*

Case 1:   During a two-week span, a police chief received five separate misconduct complaints against Officer Smith; four of the cases involve malicious or threatening conduct toward civilians. Investigations confirmed the misconduct, and Smith's district commander recommended he be discharged. The police chief immediately asked the Police Board to terminate Smith but otherwise took no action, pending the Board's decision.

During this time, while on duty, Smith attacked and beat a civilian named Jones. Jones brings a Section 1983 action against the chief, asking that he be held liable for failing to train, supervise, or discipline Smith, thus causing the injuries to Jones.

Should the police chief be liable?

Decision: _____Yes_____

Reasons: _____He should have ordered Smith suspended, or relegated to office work for protection of civilians_____

Case 2: Ben D. Law, an inmate, filed a Section 1983 suit against the commissioner and the warden after being held thirty-two days in a "strip cell," furnished only with a toilet and washbowl. In addition, he was not provided soap, towels, or toilet paper and was forced to remain nude in the cell. During the trial to determine whether the inmate's constitutional rights were violated, the warden and commissioner argued that they shouldn't be held liable because they weren't responsible for putting the inmate in the cell and that lower prison officials were directly responsible for the segregation and the inmate's treatment. They also stated that they weren't aware of the conditions in the strip cells.

However, testimony showed that the warden knew that clothing was sometimes taken from inmates in the strip cells and that the cells had only the "bare necessities." Also, Ben had sent a letter to the commissioner of corrections in which he detailed the conditions in the strip cell. The commissioner testified he referred the matter to the warden.

Should the warden be liable for any injuries to the inmate?

What about the commissioner?

Decision: Warden _____Yes_____ Commissioner _____Yes_____

Reasons: _____

_____

Case 3: Former inmate Purdy Lee Spackle filed a Section 1983 suit against Warden Lawrence Nitenjail and Chief Classification Officer Coral Reefer after it was determined that he served an additional 366 days because a conviction against another Purdy Spackle was erroneously added to Purdy Lee's sentence. He would also have sued Virgil "Numbers" Choate, the prison timekeeper, who had made the mistake, but Choate had since died.

Evidence proved that Spackle had written Nitenjail about the mix-up and that Nitenjail contacted Reefer, who stated that she was aware of the problem and was going to take care of it. Reefer asked Choate to recheck Spackle's time and was later advised by Choate that it was correct. Reefer conveyed this information directly to Spackle, who still maintained that Choate was wrong. Both Nitenjail and Reefer testified that they relied on Choate.

Since it was later proved that Choate was in error, should Nitenjail and Reefer be liable for damages?

Decision   Warden: _____ Classification Chief _____

Reasons: _____

_____

_____

Case 4: M.T. Wallet sued the prison warden and the director of the Department of Corrections for injuries he received while being held in a one-man cell. Wallet had complained loudly after missing the inmates' usual morning cup of coffee. He then slapped an officer through the cell bars. The officer threw his cup of coffee on the inmate, who yelled obscenities.

The officer called for a water hose, which was directed at Wallet's head and neck. The inmate panicked and threw items such as toilet paper and cleaning agents at the officer. The officer ordered another hose, and then tear gas was used on the inmate several times. Ten minutes later, three officers entered the cell and beat Wallet with a billy club until he lost consciousness. Wallet needed sixty-nine stitches for head wounds, which the officers claimed were the result of Wallet's attacking and fighting the officers.

Neither the warden nor the director had expressly ordered the action of the officers. However, the inmate proved that seven incidents involving high-pressure hoses on inmates in one-man cells had occurred in the recent past and that the warden and director were aware of and had approved of these actions. He also proved that they had formally opposed a commission report recommending severe restrictions on the use of hoses on confined inmates. The recommendation limited the use of force on confined inmates to situations where inmates posed a threat to themselves or others.

The case against the director centered on his failure to enact a more specific rule outlining when high-pressure hoses, billy clubs, and tear gas could be used. The director, responsible for the day-to-day operations of all state prisons, had primary responsibility for implementing policies governing the treatment of inmates. The rule in place at the time of the incident with Wallet read:

> "Physical force, firearms, tear gas, mace, and other weapons for individual control will be used only when necessary to prevent escape and injury to staff, citizenry, or inmates or to prevent damage to property."

Should the warden and director be liable?

Decision: Warden _____ Director _____

Reasons: _____

Case 5: Police patrol cars chased a pick-up truck driven by a man against whom officers believed an arrest warrant would soon be issued. Gunfire erupted. The man drove onto a ranch pursued by five police cars containing the entire six-person night shift of the force.

Officers later testified that, due to darkness and rain, they did not see the house on the ranch when they arrived. The ranch foreman, who lived with his family in the house, drove to the shooting to offer his assistance. As his pick-up reached the patrol cars, officers fired on him from two sides. He got out of his truck, was shot in the back, and died. The foreman's family filed a Section 1983 lawsuit against the officers and chief of police.

At trial, there was no direct testimony of prior misconduct in the force or prior knowledge of the police chief. Testimony showed that, after the foreman's death, the chief issued no reprimands, discharges, or admissions of error.

Should the chief be liable?

Decision: _____

Reasons: _____

Protection of Inmates

It is well accepted that both federal and state correctional institutions owe a duty of protection to inmates committed to their *custody.* This duty is sometimes stated in the following language (quoted from federal law): "The Federal Bureau of Prisons shall ... (2) provide suitable quarters for and provide for the safekeeping, care and subsistence of all persons *charged* (italic added) or convicted of offenses against the United

---

National Council on Crime and Delinquency's "A Model Act for the Protection of Rights of Prisoners" *

All persons imprisoned in accordance with law shall retain all rights of an ordinary citizen, except those expressly or by necessary implication taken by law, which include ... a general healthful environment, ... and protection against any physical or psychological abuse or unnecessary indignity.

_____

* See Appendix D.

States; (3) provide for the protection, instruction, and discipline of all persons charged with or convicted of offenses against the United States." This same duty may also be established by state law or court cases.

What constitutes negligence regarding the failure to protect in an institution is often a difficult question and depends upon the facts of each case. Liability frequently turns on the issue of whether the officer's conduct constituted a failure to fulfill the duty to protect. The test the courts use is one of "reasonableness": whether the judge or jury believes the correctional officer or official acted unreasonably.

Protecting Inmates from Other Inmates   The typical failure-to-protect case involves an inmate *claim* for damages that resulted from an assault by another inmate. If the inmate claims an intentional wrong, the injured inmate may file the claim in federal or state court or, in some places, with a claims commission. Intentional failure to protect has occurred in cases in which an inmate was attacked, officers were called for help, and the officers failed to respond. A number of courts have found such intentional failure to protect to be cruel and unusual punishment that gives rise to a *constitutional claim.* This constitutional claim is an alternative to the injury claims that usually can be filed in state courts.

As most situations do not concern an intentional failure to protect, many cases claim that the official, officer, and/or institution was negligent or grossly negligent in failing to protect the inmate.

An example of the reasonableness test applied in one case of alleged negligence is as follows.

During an orientation period in the state's reformatory, Inmate Hall made sexual advances to Inmate Barnard. Without giving reasons, Barnard requested and was granted a cell change. Several days later, Hall assaulted Barnard in the dining hall with a razor blade, causing Barnard extensive injuries. Razor blades were regularly issued to inmates, one at a time, under strict supervision. Four officers intervened to stop the assault. Barnard sued the state for failing to protect him from Hall's attack.

The court said the state would be liable where it could be shown that it had unreasonably exposed inmates to risks. However, in this case, the court found no proof that the state had failed to take reasonable care for Barnard's safety and found against the inmate. The state knew of no hostility between the inmates, Hall had never caused trouble before, and quick and effective measures were taken to subdue the assault once it began.[14]

Fear of assault was enough in one case to establish a constitutional violation. Inmates were given cell keys, which were then used to open cells of other inmates for assaults, robberies, and homosexual activities. The inmate bringing suit did not have to wait until he was actually assaulted before obtaining the court's help. He was only required to show a pervasive risk of harm from other prisoners.[15]

Some courts are reluctant to find negligence unless officials knew or should have known of a dangerous situation. In one case, the court found no negligence because the officials did not know of any hostility, tension, or personal problem between the inmates prior to the attack. Some states also require a specific "danger signal" to come to the attention of employees who then fail to take adequate precautions. Other courts have said that if a correctional employee "should have known of the danger," this may be enough to establish liability.

Note that liability for failure to protect may arise not only from assaults by inmates but from assaults by other law enforcement personnel. The following case is an example.

A jailer was held liable along with a police officer for $12,000 when it was proved that the jailer watched the police officer, who had brought his prisoner to the jail, attack the prisoner. The jailer denied the inmate's request for medical care, and it was not until the jailer's shift ended ten hours later that the inmate was released to his wife. The court ruled that the jailer had a duty to protect prisoners at the jail and had allowed the beating to take place.[16]

One federal court stated the following standard for determining when correctional supervisors may be liable. The court did not look for knowledge of the specific danger by the administrators but rather said it must decide: "(1) whether there is a pervasive risk of harm to inmates from other prisoners and, if so (2) whether the officials are exercising reasonable care to prevent prisoners from intentionally harming others or from creating an unreasonable risk of harm." [17] The question will usually be: Did the official (e.g., the sheriff or warden) act reasonably in attempting to correct the situation? Correctional officials will not be held liable if they did all they could or if what happened was totally out of their control.

Problem 12

An inmate in a jail was awaiting admission to a state mental hospital. After being found guilty by a group of inmates of being an informer, he was tied to his cell by other inmates, burned with cigarettes, and homosexually raped. He suffered a fractured skull, ribs, jaw, a broken nose, and dozens of abrasions. Evidence indicated that patrols of the cellblock did not take place during the attack, prisoners were not segregated, and cell locks were broken. Should the county be liable for the inmate's injuries?

Problem 13

Inmate Gomez reached for a gun and then was shot to death by Inmate Warren. Gomez's estate sued the state for creating a situation where inmates could carry guns despite prison regulations prohibiting them. Should the state be liable?

Protecting Inmates from Themselves   In a number of recent cases, the claim has been made that institutions must protect inmates, especially those under the influence of drugs or alcohol or who are suffering from mental problems, from inflicting wounds on themselves or committing suicide. The courts have differed in their judgments in these cases. Some courts have stated that suicide or suicide attempts are intentional acts by inmates and that inmates should not profit from their own wrongdoing. Other courts have placed liability on the correctional personnel based on the fact that an institution's duty of care should be even greater for those under the influence of drugs or alcohol or who are mentally ill.

Walker was being held in a city's "drunk tank." Another intoxicated person, Smith, was placed in the same holding cell. Almost immediately and without reason, he punched and kicked Walker. Another inmate, fearing for his own safety, pounded on the window of the tank and yelled for help, but the jailers did not respond. Smith, a former professional prizefighter and escapee from a mental institution, dropped Walker on his head. Walker never recovered and can no longer talk or reason. Walker was discovered sometime later when the jailer admitted another drunk. The officers involved and the city were *held* negligent and ordered to pay $200,000 in damages. The jailer testified that fighting was to be expected among the drunks and that the jail rules required hourly physical inspections, as well as constant television and audio monitoring. The state court held that the failure to conduct such inspections and respond to the inmate's call constituted negligence. The court also noted that the jailer owed Walker a higher degree of care because of his intoxicated state.[18]

Where institutions have no written standards for handling special prisoners, such as alcohol abusers or the mentally ill, some courts have applied standards to them.

Parsons, an inmate with a history of mental illness, was being held in a local jail. He was examined by a psychiatrist who advised that Parsons should be admitted immediately to a mental hospital to protect himself and others. This advice was not immediately followed, but Parsons was segregated in a cell with a small window through which officers could observe him. He was allowed to retain his matches and cigarettes.

Parsons "heard voices" and set his mattress and hair on fire to scare them away. He suffered severe burns and had to have five fingers amputated.

Parsons sued, and the court awarded him $117,000 because of the jail employees' negligence. The jail had no written standards for guiding its personnel in handling prisoners with mental problems, and the court accepted expert testimony that hospitals in the area followed specific procedures with someone in Parsons' condition. These included continuous observations, stripping of personal effects, dressing the patient in a hospital gown with no cord, and placing the patient in a room with no overhanging pipes.[19]

Problem 14

A seventeen-year-old boy tried to escape from a youth facility and was caught and transferred to an isolation cell. He attempted to commit

suicide, was found shortly thereafter, but had already suffered irreparable brain damage. The facility had a behavior-modification program that involved punishing a group of inmates for the antics of one of its members. Evidence showed that this system of punishment had driven the boy to a state of extreme depression, which the court found was foreseeable on the part of the state. The court also ruled that the conditions in the isolation cell amounted to cruel and unusual punishment. Because of these findings, should the state be liable to the boy and his parents?

Protection and Classification A key issue in situations where inmates are attacked by others or harm themselves may be the classification process within the institution. For example, if classification officers and/or officials knew or should have known that an inmate would be in danger if placed in a certain cellblock but still placed him there and he was killed, they might be found liable in a later lawsuit. Likewise, if a known suicide risk was classified and placed in an area where there was little observation or separation from dangerous instruments and if the inmate stabbed himself, it is possible that a lawsuit and liability might result. One inmate received $250 because his cell assignment was based solely upon his race.[20]

Classification Standards *

5335. There is a written plan for classifying inmates in terms of level of custody required, housing assignment and participation in correctional programs.

5336. The written plan for inmate classification specifies criteria and procedures for determining and changing the status of an inmate, including custody, transfers and major changes in programs.

5337. The facility provides for the separate management of the following categories of inmates:

Unsentenced females;

Sentenced females;

Unsentenced males;

Sentenced males;

Other classes of detainees, e.g., witnesses, civil prisoners;

Community custody inmates, e.g., work releasees, weekenders, trustees;

Inmates with special problems, e.g., alcoholics, narcotics addicts, mentally disturbed persons, physically handicapped persons, persons with communicable diseases;

Inmates requiring disciplinary detention;

Inmates requiring administrative segregation;

and Juveniles.

5338. Juveniles in custody are provided living quarters separate from adult inmates, although these may be in the same structure. (Detention—Essential, Holding—Essential)

5339. Female inmates are provided living quarters separate from male inmates, although these may be in the same structure.

5340. Written policy and procedure specify an appeals process for classification decisions.

5341. Written policy and procedure prohibit segregation of inmates by race, color, creed or national origin.

5342. Male and female inmates have equal access to all programs and activities.

---

* *Manual of Standards for Adult Local Detention Facilities,* Commission on Accreditation for Corrections, (1977), pp. 70–71. Reprinted with the permission of the American Correctional Association.

The standards developed by the American Correctional Association for Classification in Adult Local Detention Facilities are on p. 48. Most of these standards would be applicable to prisons as well.

Problem 15 ◆ Classification Roleplay *

Assume that your institution has minimum security (dormitories), medium (cell blocks holding four persons each), maximum (single-person cells), and lockup (no interaction with other inmates) and that the following four people are sitting on a classification committee for new inmates:

- ◆ Deputy warden/security,
- ◆ Deputy warden/treatment programs,
- ◆ Institutional nurse, and
- ◆ Industrial shopkeeper.

One person should play each of these persons at a classification committee meeting for a new inmate, George Beam, who may be present at the entire meeting or called in for part of it by the committee. Each participant should represent the typical viewpoint of a person in his or her position and then come to a decision on Beam's classification.

Case History

Inmate Name	—George Beam # 77805, Age 31
Sentenced	—2 years
Charge	—Carnal knowledge of female minor (has prior cases of this type)
Education	—Has I.Q. of 110. Two years of college, five years of machine-shop experience. Has excellent employment record. (Inmates in maximum or lockup may not work in the vocational programs.)
Social	—Reports state that Beam is a loner. His outward appearance is poor. During Beam's pre-sentence status, he was harassed by peer inmates and, at one point, "snitched" on a fellow inmate. This snitching resulted in several inmates in this institution (in medium security) receiving strong disciplinary sentences.
Medical	—Beam has made several suicide attempts. On his last attempt three months ago, first-aid was necessary to

revive him. Beam still shows signs of depression.

* Adapted with permission from a roleplay developed by William Gimignani and Samuel Coleman, trainers from the New Haven (Connecticut) Corrections Center.

Escapes

In some instances, escapes occur due to negligence on the part of correctional employees. The inmate who escapes may commit a second crime, and the victim of the crime may have a right to claim damages against the correctional employees who allowed the escape.

An inmate who had escaped from a local jail fired a rifle through a window, injuring a woman inside. The victim filed suit, and the court stated that the jail employees' negligence in not providing proper security in the institution could make them liable to compensate the woman for her damages. The principal issue in a situation like this is whether the injury occurring in the street was "a probable and foreseeable consequence" of the escape.[21]

Problem 16

A jail's rules require that all visitors be searched before entering the institution. Correctional Officer Willard, who is working the gate, fails to search a visitor. It is later shown that a gun was brought into the institution by the visitor and given to an inmate who then was able to escape. During the escape, an innocent bystander was shot. Could Officer Willard be held liable for this act? What if Willard's supervisor or the jail manager knew Willard often neglected to search, but they did nothing about it?

Duty to Warn

The general rule is that individuals have no duty to warn others of possible dangers unless there is a *special* relationship. What does it take to establish such a special relationship? The several courts that have answered this question seem to say that there are three requirements.

First, there must be a foreseeable victim or specific group at risk who is readily identifiable. The group at risk has to be sufficiently small so that a warning would make a difference. If every young boy is at risk, the group is not sufficiently identifiable, and there would be no special relationship.

Second, the harm must be foreseeable. For example, it is foreseeable that a person with convictions for child molestations might molest children in a day-care center. It is not foreseeable that a person with convictions for child molestations would embezzle money from a bank. Generally, foreseeable harm is made known through past history or from specific threats. Also, the foreseeable harm must not be easily discoverable by the endangered persons.

Third, there must be dependence or reliance. Generally, this means that the victim must have been put into a more vulnerable position because of the actions of another. For example, when an officer obtains a job in a pharmacy for an inmate with a history of drug usage without informing the employer, the employer relies upon the officer.

When a special relationship exists, an individual must warn the intended victim of the potential danger. If no warning occurs and a foreseeable harm occurs to a foreseeable victim, then liability may exist for damages resulting from the injury.

Problem 17

Directions: Decide whether or not there is a special relationship in each of the following cases that would justify a duty to warn.

A. Mrs. Johnson was attacked by a minor placed in her foster home by the Youth Authority, which gave no warning that the minor had known homicidal tendencies.

B. Mr. Poddar made threats against Ms. Tarasoff during his psychotherapy sessions. He later kills the woman, and her family sues the psychotherapist for failing to take reasonable steps to protect their daughter.

C. The county paroled a juvenile offender who indicated he intended to harm young children. He went to live with his mother, and, within four days of his release, he killed a young boy in a nearby apartment.

D. Mrs. Davidson was stabbed in a public laundromat under surveillance by police. The police were trying to prevent assaults and apprehend a man who had stabbed women on three earlier occasions in the laundromat. The officers were aware of Mrs. Davidson in the laundromat. They saw a man on the premises and, after watching him for fifteen minutes, identified him as the likely perpetrator of an assault the night before. The officers did not warn Mrs. Davidson, who was stabbed by the suspect.

E. Probationer Klein got a job on his own efforts as an assistant to the president of JAMCO and was named executive vice president two months later. At the time he was hired, he was on probation following a criminal conviction for larceny and embezzlement. The probationer informed his probation officers that he had a sales position with JAMCO and that he had not told his new employer of his criminal history and probationary status. When the officers verified Klein's employment, they did not reveal Klein's status. Klein embezzled $100,000 from JAMCO.

F. On May 2, 1980, Mr. Johnson, who was driving on the wrong side of the freeway, was arrested by sheriff's officers. Upon his arrest, he told them he was attempting to commit suicide, that "people were trying to torture and kill" him, and he pleaded that the officers kill him. Mr. Johnson was charged with assault with a deadly weapon and taken into custody.

Shortly thereafter, Mr. Johnson's wife informed the officers that her husband was a paranoid schizophrenic, had been repeatedly hospitalized, and required immediate medication (Thorazine) to correct a chemical imbalance that caused his bizarre behavior. She further said that Mr. Johnson had suicidal tendencies requiring immediate medical attention and should not be released. The officers acknowledged that Mr. Johnson required medical attention, promised to hospitalize and medicate him, and advised his wife not to worry.

On May 5, 1980, Mr. Johnson was released from the county jail without notice to his wife; on May 7, he committed suicide.

Should the sheriff and his officers be liable for failure to warn Mrs. Johnson of Mr. Johnson's pending release?

Fires

When a fire occurs in a correctional institution and inmates are injured or killed, it is likely that lawsuits will result. The usual claim in these cases is that negligence on the part of correctional employees was the reasonable and foreseeable cause *(proximate cause)* of the fire. This means it must be proven that what the correctional employees did or failed to do was the direct cause of the fire and the resulting injuries. In some cases, the local fire department may also be named a defendant. Common types of claims have been that the fire or injuries occurred because of:

◆ poor conditions in the institution, such as improper ventilation or unsatisfactory means of exit from rooms of confinement;

◆ careless storage of dangerous liquids;

◆ lack of adequate procedures;

◆ improper training of correctional officers in fire fighting or in emergency procedures;

◆ failure to make regular checks on prisoners or failure to inspect safety devices routinely;

◆ incorrect stationing of officers; or

◆ incomplete searches of inmates.

In fire cases, courts have not always decided against corrections employees. In many cases, it has been shown that the fire was caused by the negligence of an inmate and was not the result of actions by corrections employees. In such cases, the employees have not been held liable.

Although a fire may never occur, it is best to prevent fires by examining the present conditions in a jail or prison.

Problem 18

A fire broke out in a cellblock and injured a number of inmates. A case was filed, and, at the trial, it was shown that the correctional officer with the key to the main door of the cellblock was located in another building, 300 yards away. Who could be held liable for the injuries incurred?

False Imprisonment

Under the law in most states, and pursuant to the Federal Civil Rights Act, a person who is either falsely arrested or imprisoned has the right to file a suit for damages against the person or persons—or in some places, the government agency—that caused the false imprisonment.

Checklist of Fire Hazards in Institutions *

1. Are the cells "fireproof" in design and construction?

2. Will the ventilation system vacate smoke, noxious gases, and flames, or will it spread them?

3. Are mattresses and clothing that are provided fully fireproof or only flame resistant? At what sustained temperature will they burn on their own? What tests have been conducted by the manufacturer or independent laboratories? Are mattresses promptly replaced when the covers are torn?

4. Are fire, smoke, and gas sensors installed? Ionization chamber sensors are the first to respond but cannot be used in furnace rooms and some laundry areas, where photoelectric-eye smoke detectors must be used. Thermal (heat sensitive) detectors should be used in the facility's kitchen and lounge areas where smoking is allowed.

5. Is the alarm system independent of the institution's electrical system? Are there sufficient bells or horns in the institution and lights in the communications room?

6. Is there a master system for unlocking cellblocks in times of disaster? Are there sufficient extra keys for manual operation of cell doors for a mass exodus if the master system fails?

7. Are there sufficient escape routes? Are they well marked and compartmentalized or protected by sprinklers? Is there a battery-operated emergency lighting system in all corridors?

8. Are there enough standpipes, fire hoses, and extinguishers? Are there several smoke masks or facial air packs? Does every correctional officer have a set of keys to fire-suppression-equipment cabinets?

9. Are officers taught fire-suppression techniques? Have they rehearsed evacuations in regularly scheduled drills?

10. Is there a sufficient number of officers on duty to prevent or quickly detect fires? If not, have remote-controlled closed-circuit televisions been installed?

11. Are frequent inspections made to insure that all equipment is properly functioning, that torn mattresses are not accessible to inmates, and that other problems are prevented?

---

* Adapted from *AELE Jail and Prisoner Law Bulletin,* with permission. Sample issues may be obtained from AELE, 5519 N. Cumberland Ave., Suite 1008, Chicago, IL 60656.

To win a false imprisonment suit against corrections employees, negligence or intentional action that resulted in the unfair imprisonment must be shown. Therefore, if it can be shown that a jailer mixed up the records of one inmate with another and that, consequently, an inmate was held for a longer period than legally permitted, the jailer may be held liable for damages. It should be noted that usually the present law allows corrections employees to raise the defense of "good faith": If it can be demonstrated that the employee was acting reasonably and that the error took place outside his or her area of responsibility, the employee will not be liable.

Problem 19

County Sheriff Brown received notice from the District Attorney's office that one *indictment* against Inmate Caulfield had been dismissed but that another indictment against Caulfield was still in effect. The second notice was in error, and Caulfield was improperly held for thirty-six days in the county jail. Who could be held liable for this error?

Medical Treatment

Under local, state, and federal law, correctional facilities are required to provide adequate medical treatment to inmates in their custody. Treatment must be provided for serious medical needs inmates had when they entered the institution or developed after they were there. The duty also includes care provided after an operation.[22]

Failure to provide treatment in accordance with general medical practices may constitute negligence and give rise to a tort case in a state court against the doctor, the correctional employees involved, and/or the institution or other governmental unit. Inmates may also be able to file a suit in federal court claiming a violation of a constitutional right, but the U.S. Supreme Court has ruled that more than negligence must be proved to establish that medical treatment supports a "cruel and unusual punishment" constitutional claim. The court has held that inmates may sue in federal court only if there was "deliberate indifference to (their) serious medical needs." (See pp. 107–108)

Medical personnel sometimes commit a special kind of negligence, called medical *malpractice.* This occurs when, under all circumstances, they fail to exercise the degree of skill and learning commonly applied in the community by the average, prudent, reputable member of the profession, and there is a resulting injury.

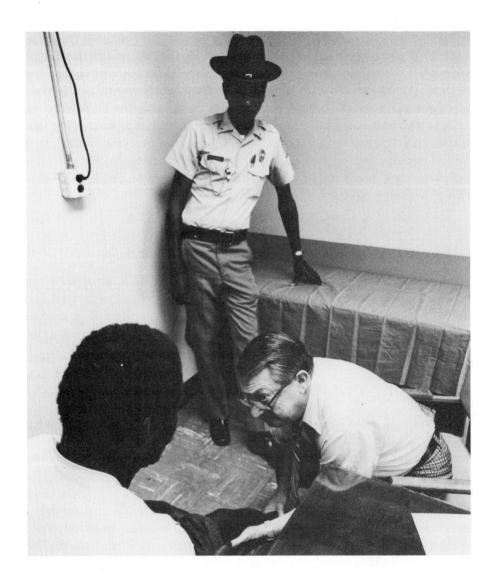

This definition of malpractice has at least two important components that should be highlighted: community and average. The standard of care is what is average in the particular community where the medical personnel provide their services. This means that standards of care may and will vary, depending upon the location of the medical providers.

For security staff to be liable in the delivery of medical care, inmates must prove either that staff members were "deliberately indifferent to their serious medical needs" or that personnel acted negligently. For instance, an officer collects "sick call slips" and accidentally loses one on the way to the medical office. If the inmate suffers greater medical problems because of the delay, this is negligence. Other examples of negligence would be if an officer failed to put an inmate on light-duty status after a doctor has ordered it, with a resulting aggravation of medical problems, or if officers removed an inmate from a hospital against the doctor's orders and without a hospital release.

A common question is: May security officers, without training, hand out medications to inmates? The answer is not clear. If unit dosages are prepackaged by medical staff and if the health authority plans to use officers as deliverers, there may be no problem. A protocol or medical procedure established by the medical authority (doctor) should include defined procedures on dispensing, administering, and distributing medicines that comply with state law and applicable case decisions.

If the system established by the health authority is likely to create error, there can be liability. However, line officers, who follow written policies that they are not likely to know are defective, would not be held personally liable.

Some courts have held that, if two doctors disagree about appropriate medical care and if the warden follows the advice of one in providing a specific type of medical care, this action will be viewed as a medical difference of opinion, and the warden will not be held liable. However, this does not mean that the doctor could not be held liable if his or her advice was found to constitute medical malpractice. Under certain conditions, the county or state government can also be held liable for a doctor's negligent action.

Frequently, inmates complain about the quality of health care, including such problems as long lines and waiting periods, foreign staff who can't understand and speak fluent English, staff whose attitudes indicate a disrespect for inmates, inappropriate treatment, insufficient use of diagnostic tests, and lack of feedback on tests. These problems are usually not serious enough to constitute "cruel and unusual punishment" or medical malpractice, especially if no specific harm can be shown, but some courts have begun to look more closely at quality-of-care issues and sometimes issue broad orders to improve medical practices.

May an inmate refuse medical treatment? May an inmate be forced to submit to a medical examination upon admission to an institution? The general rule for inmates is the same as that for persons on the outside: A doctor may not treat a competent adult until the treatment, its risks, alternatives, and success rates have been explained to the patient, and the patient's consent has been given. This rule is primarily based on the constitutional right to privacy.[23]

This general rule has some exceptions: (1) where the state can show some compelling state interest in administering the treatment; (2) where the adult is not competent; or (3) in emergency situations where consent can be implied.

Because the state has a valid interest in stopping the spread of communicable diseases, it could justify giving shots for contagious diseases despite a person's refusal.[24] The institution's duty to provide for the safety of its inmates could justify the requirement that all submit to physical examinations by a doctor upon admission.

As stated earlier in this chapter, the state has a duty to protect inmates from themselves. Correctional personnel, when confronted with an attempted suicide victim, do not have to allow the inmate to die if he or she refuses medical treatment. In some cases, the courts have permitted institutions to give forced treatment on the grounds that the refusing victim is not mentally competent, and/or the giving of medical treatment in such a case is sufficiently related to the security needs of the institution.[25] Also, in emergency situations, such as when an inmate is unconscious, treatment may be given.[26]

Hunger strikes present a unique situation to which courts have responded inconsistently. On the one hand, expressions of political and religious beliefs merit First Amendment protections (See chapter 3, Prisoners' Rights), but institutions also have a duty of care owed to inmates in their custody. Inmates also have a right of privacy over intrusions into their bodies.

Most courts that have addressed forced feeding of inmates on hunger strikes have ruled that inmates may be force-fed when their physical condition deteriorates to a point that is life threatening.[27] However, at least one state supreme court refused to permit forced feeding and involuntary medical treatment of a competent inmate who had no dependents relying upon him for support. The inmate had claimed he was making an attempt for a transfer out of a state because of plans to kill him in that state. The state supreme court ruled that the right to privacy prevented forced feeding, monitoring his condition against his will, or preventing his death by suicide.[28]

An area of law that needs special attention is the right of an inmate to refuse psychotropic medication. Psychotropic medication includes antipsychotics, lithium, and antidepressants, but the present controversy surrounds the right to refuse antipsychotic medications. Some brand names of the common antipsychotic medications are Dazoline, Haldol, Inapsine, Lidone, Loxitane, Mellaril, Moban, Navane, Permitil, Prolixin, Quide, Serentil, Serpasil, Stelazine, Taractan, Thorazine, Tindal, Trilafon, and Vesprin.

Inmates might want to refuse these medications because the side effects are severe. Muscular side effects include muscle spasms, especially in the eyes, neck, face, and arms; irregular flexing; tongue protrusion; restlessness and agitation; muscle stiffness and rigidity. Nonmuscular side effects include drowsiness, weariness, weakness; weight gain; dizziness; stuffy nose; dry mouth; low blood pressure; lowered body temperature; apathy; depression; loss of sexual desire and inability to have an erection or orgasm; constipation; difficult urination; sensitivity to sunlight; skin discoloration; cessation of menstruation; and secretion of breast milk.

The most serious side effect is a disease called tardive dyskinesia, which damages the body's nervous system. The only known way to get this incurable disease is by taking antipsychotic drugs. Signs of tardive dyskinesia include constant movement of the lips, tongue, hands, or fingers. This may cause smacking or puckering of the lips, moving the tongue back and forth, puffing the cheeks, or chewing. The body may be involuntarily twisted into unusual positions that prevent a person from walking or resting normally.

The symptoms of tardive dyskinesia often are undetectable until a person has stopped taking the medications. Some experts believe that 10 to 20 percent of all hospitalized mental patients have this disease.

Inmates base their challenge to forced antipsychotic medications on several constitutional rights: the right to privacy, including the right to make one's own decisions about fundamental matters; the due process right to personal dignity and bodily integrity; and the First Amendment right to communicate ideas freely.

On the other hand, jail and prison personnel justify their authority to force an inmate to take properly prescribed antipsychotic medication on three principles. The first is their right and duty to treat mentally ill persons in their custody. The second principle is the jail's interest in maintaining pretrial detainees in a competent condition to stand trial. Thirdly, their justification is based on the institution's duty to maintain security and to prevent violent and dangerous mentally ill prisoners from injuring themselves or others.

The courts balance the rights and interests on each side to determine what action should be taken in each particular setting. Some courts have held that only an emergency could justify such involuntary administration of antipsychotics.

This emergency requires a professional judgment call that includes balancing the institution's concerns for the safety of its occupants against an inmate's interest in freedom from unwanted antipsychotics. The decision to medicate must be the product of professional judgment by appropriate medical authorities, applying accepted medical standards. It requires an evaluation in each case of all the relevant circumstances, including the nature and gravity of the safety threat, the characteristics of the individual involved, and the likely effects of particular drugs. Also, the availability of alternative, less-restrictive courses of action, such as segregation or the use of less controversial drugs such as tranquilizers or sedatives, has to be considered.[29]

Problem 20

An inmate's glasses were broken during a scuffle, although he was an innocent bystander. Despite repeated requests, including a letter to the warden, the inmate was not examined for three months, at which time the physician found the inmate's vision to have been permanently impaired. Who could be held liable for this injury?

Problem 21

Some people have argued that, because inmates are in the custody of the government, when they are hurt by anyone—be it another inmate or a correctional officer—they should receive compensation to make up for this loss. This is similar to workers' compensation for employees and might be paid with insurance carried by the jail or prison.

  A. What would be the arguments against this?

  B. Would this be better than the present system of compensating injuries? Explain.

  C. If this system awarded an inmate a set amount of money—say, $5,000 in a medical malpractice case—could inmates argue they were being treated unfairly and discriminated against?

INJURIES AND LOSSES TO JAIL AND PRISON PERSONNEL

As an employee of a governmental unit, the correctional employee is likely to be the *beneficiary* of certain types of insurance policies covering medical costs and paying benefits upon the employee's death (life insurance). In addition to these benefits, employees may also be the beneficiaries of certain other types of insurance.

Life Insurance

Under regulations implemented by the U.S. Department of Justice in accord with the Public Safety Officers' Act of 1976, an officer's family may be eligible to receive $50,000 if he or she is killed in the line of duty, if the death is the direct result of an injury sustained while working and if the deceased was a "law enforcement officer" as that phrase is defined in state statutes or the applicable job description.[30]

1. Line of Duty. The Justice Department defines "line of duty" as follows: "Any action which an officer is obligated or authorized by rule, regulation, condition of employment or service or law to perform, including those social, ceremonial or athletic functions to which he is assigned, or for which he is compensated, by the public agency he serves." Note that this definition does include females and does not require that employees be engaged in hazardous duty; nor does it require that they be engaged directly in crime control.

2. Cause of Death. As previously noted, for coverage under the act, the death must have been the result of an injury sustained on the job. An "injury" is defined as: "A traumatic event, caused by extensive force, including injuries inflicted by bullets, explosives, sharp instruments, blunt objects or other physical blows, chemicals, electricity, climatic conditions, infectious disease and bacteria, but not those caused by stress and strain." Note that coverage is in effect even if the injury was deliberately inflicted on the officer by a third person.

3. Law Enforcement Officer. A "law enforcement officer" is defined as any person who is "involved in crime and deliquency control or reduction, or enforcement of the criminal laws." The dead person need not have had the authority to enforce all criminal laws.

Workers' Compensation

As employees, correctional personnel may be covered under a workers' compensation policy. As a general rule, workers' compensation statutes have the following effect: If employees are injured (not killed) on the job, there is a duty to pay a prescribed amount of money. Payments are usually made under an insurance policy purchased by the employer. The favorable part of such a system is that employees are paid compensation for the injury whether or not the employer was at fault. In other words, negligence by the employer need not be proven. If an employee is injured while working and the employee is covered under workers' compensation, a certain amount of money will be paid.

On the other hand, in most jurisdictions the existence of workers' compensation makes it impossible to sue the employer unless the employer has committed an intentional act or omission. In other words, if the employee is injured on the job, the employee may apply only for workers' compensation, even if the prescribed payments are far less than what the employee might recover from the court if he or she sued the employer. Some states give greater protection, covering occupational diseases or death that result from activities in the course of employment.

Compensation for Property Losses

Assume an inmate assaults a correctional employee and breaks her glasses. Will the state pay for a new pair of glasses? States have different answers to this question. Many times, a commission or board has the authority to pay money to replace such items up to a certain dollar amount. Some states cover this type of loss in their workers' compensation policy. Other institutions may pay for the item out of supplies or petty cash. The employee may also be able to sue the inmate in a small-claims court. Other states have a policy that the job assumes certain risks and that there is no *remedy* for such losses.

RIGHT TO BE FREE FROM JOB DISCRIMINATION

Under federal law, employers of fifteen or more persons (with certain exceptions) are prohibited from discriminating on the basis of race, color, religion, sex, or national origin. Discrimination is banned in hiring, firing, paying, classifying, training, apprenticing, referring for employment, and in union membership.

An "employer" includes state and local governments and governmental agencies (except in the District of Columbia). Since the state Department of Corrections is a state agency, it is an employer that may not discriminate under the federal law. Likewise, a local jail will be subject to this law if it has fifteen or more employees.

If a correctional officer believes that his or her employer has discriminated on any of the grounds listed here, the officer must file a charge with the federal Equal Employment Opportunity Commission. A suit in federal court cannot be brought until the charge has been filed and the EEOC has acted or has issued a "letter to sue."

However, most states also have their own equal employment practices agencies to protect their citizens from discrimination. Generally, a discrimination charge must first be filed with the state agency and then with the EEOC. Strict time limits for filing must be met.

The state statute may prohibit discrimination in employment for reasons in addition to race, color, sex, religion, and national origin. For example, a state law may also prohibit discrimination on the basis of age, marital status, political affiliation, sexual orientation, physical handicap, and so on.

Why are some regulations or acts by employers permitted under the law even though they clearly treat persons differently based on factors prohibited by the law? Why, for instance, did the Supreme Court in 1976 say that the Alabama Department of Corrections could make a rule keeping female correctional officers out of "contact positions" with male inmates? [31]

The answer is that certain acts that ordinarily constitute discrimination fall within the exceptions to the law. The relevant exceptions to the federal law are (1) *bona fide* occupational qualification, or BFOQ, and (2) the results of a professionally developed ability test, so long as the test is not designed to discriminate.

The BFOQ applies only to discrimination based on sex, religion, and national origin (not to race and color) where the discrimination is reasonably necessary for the normal operation of that business. For instance, if a Kosher meat processor had a practice of hiring only Jews to kill the livestock, this would appear to be employment discrimination based on religion. If it was admitted that only Jews were being hired, one could argue that being Jewish was a BFOQ for a Kosher meat processor and was reasonably necessary to the normal operation of the business.

The Alabama example previously mentioned was a unique situation in which the court found that being a male was a BFOQ for contact positions in this maximum-security prison. The court found that male sex offenders were housed throughout the population and that women officers were likely to be raped, thus creating an even worse atmosphere.

Many correctional agencies designate positions as BFOQ male or BFOQ female. Employers, unions, employees, and inmates have challenged these BFOQ designations under different theories. Employers assert their duty to provide secure institutions. The unions and employees assert their rights to job benefits (promotions, overtime, preferred shifts, etc.) that may be denied when jobs are designated as BFOQ. Inmates claim the right to be free from observation by the opposite sex when undressing, using the toilets, being strip searched, and in other situations. They claim such exposure is humiliating and degrading and in violation of their constitutional right to privacy.

What can the employer do? Should it refuse to hire females for male institutions and males for female institutions? Females claim that this would not be a fair resolution, since 90 percent of all inmates are male, and only 10 percent of all inmates are female. Additionally, officers claim they are quite competent to perform the job of correctional officer in either male or female institutions.

Although the Supreme Court has not made a ruling on these conflicting interests, lower courts have ruled on this question in several cases.

There was initially a trend to enforce selective work assignments so that officers of the opposite sex would not work in areas during times that inmates' privacy might be invaded. The court decisions appear now to be weighed more in favor of protecting officer employment rights over privacy of inmates while providing for institutional security.[32]

For instance, in one recent case, the court ruled that the prison officials had struck an acceptable balance among the male prisoners' privacy interests, the institution's security requirements, and the female officers' employment rights by generally assigning female officers to posts where they have a distant or obstructed view of inmates. Inmates' rights were not violated when females conducted pat-down searches or viewed strip searches in emergency situations.[33]

In three Federal District Court rulings, judges have ruled that there is no federal constitutional right to privacy involved in opposite-sex supervision of inmates. Two of these cases are unreported. However, the reported case ruled that female officers could perform clothed, pat-down searches of males, including the anal-genital area, and could observe males showering and using the toilets.[34]

Some experts now claim that the social experiment of using female officers in male institutions reveals that females contribute to the normality of the prison and foster rehabilitation. Also inmates apparently feel comfortable with opposite-sex supervision as long as the officer behaves professionally and as long as there are methods for preserving the inmates' modesty.[35]

In recent years, there have been numerous lawsuits claiming a particular type of sex discrimination under Title VII—that of sexual harassment.

The Equal Employment Opportunity Commission defines sexual harassment in three ways: unwelcome sexual advances, requests for sexual favors, and other verbal or physical conduct of a sexual nature when (1) submission to such conduct is made either explicitly or implicitly a term or condition of an individual's employment, (2) submission to or rejection of such conduct by an individual is used as the basis for employment decisions affecting such an individual, or (3) such conduct has the purpose or effect of unreasonably interfering with an individual's work performance or creating an intimidating, hostile, or offensive work environment.[36]

The employer is liable for sexual harassment committed by a supervisor when the employer knows or reasonably should have known of that harassment. Employers are also liable for sexual harassment directed against an employee by a nonsupervisory co-employee where the employer knew or should have known of the harassment unless the employer can demonstrate that it took immediate and appropriate corrective action.[37]

There are even times when the employer may be responsible when nonemployees sexually harass employees in the workplace, where the employer knew or should have known of the harassment and failed to take immediate and appropriate action. The extent of the employer's control over the nonemployee's action will be considered.[38] Hypothetically, an employer could be liable for sex harassment committed by vendors who come into the institution and sexually harass an officer. The officer would have to complain to the supervisor, who then does nothing to stop the harassment. An employer might also be liable if an officer complained of an inmate's harassment and no action were taken.

In 1986, the U.S. Supreme Court addressed the issue of sexual harassment for the first time. In that case:

A former bank employee claimed she had been sexually harassed by a supervisor in connection with her job. She said she had voluntarily engaged in sexual relations with her supervisor for fear of losing her job and that the supervisor had also fondled her in the office and committed other acts of harassment.

Though she did not lose her job or claim economic loss, she asked the court to declare the hostile environment and resulting negative psychological effects on her to be tantamount to "sexual harassment."

The U.S. Supreme Court unanimously ruled that proving the existence of a hostile or abusive work environment was enough to establish a "sexual harassment" claim under Title 7 of the Employment Discrimination Law. Since 1980, the Equal Employment Opportunity Commission had declared sexual harassment itself a violation of the Act and has issued guidelines. The Court said the act "must be severe or pervasive sufficiently to alter the conditions of the victim's employment and create an abusive working environment." It also said that, depending on the circumstances, "the employer may be liable for the employee's misconduct."[39]

The Case of Female Inmate Privacy

Female inmates sue the institution and the employee union, complaining that the assignment of male correctional officers to the housing areas violates their constitutional right to privacy.

Male officers have obtained work assignments in the housing area as a result of the Equal Employment Opportunity Act ban on discrimination on the basis of sex. Women inmates are assigned to cells that have a nine-by-six-inch window in the cell door with the interior of the cell, including bed and toilet, visible to any person standing at the window.

Male officers can and have viewed them (1) in their cells in states of partial and total nudity during dressing and undressing, while sleeping, and while using the toilet; (2) in the shower, where only a shoulder-height partition blocks the direct view of the officers; and (3) in the infirmary, in states of complete or partial nudity.

During the day hours only, the women are allowed to request paper to cover their cell window for a fifteen-minute period during which they have absolute privacy.

Trial Judge Analysis

Men and women from the beginning of recorded history have a basic need for privacy in certain areas of living. Invasions of privacy cause shame and embarrassment. While an inmate's privacy must be limited in the interest of security, a right to privacy still exists in the institution.

The job of correctional officer can be performed equally well by any qualified and trained man or woman, so the positions must be open to either under the Equal Employment Opportunity Act.

Court Ruled

The court ruled that the following were impermissible invasions of privacy.

1. During the day, an inmate should not be forced to be observed while using the toilet or go where she may or must risk being viewed completely or partly in the nude by a male officer in the course of his duties.

2. During the night, she should not be observed by male officers when she uses the toilet or sleeps.

3. An inmate should not be directly observable by a male officer while she is taking a shower.

4. A male officer in the hospital should not be so stationed as to permit him, under normal circumstances, to view an inmate wholly or partly unclothed.

Question

How would you comply with the order and not violate employees' rights?

How do people prove that illegal discrimination has been practiced against them? For example, a correctional officer believes he did not get a promotion to lieutenant because he is black. It is almost impossible to get those who made the promotion to admit that their decision was due to discrimination. Therefore, the courts permit the use of statistics to prove that discrimination has occurred. The black officer, or his attorney, may be able to obtain statistics from the officer's performance evaluation to determine whether whites with worse records were being promoted or whether black and white officers as groups receive different rates of promotion based on their performance evaluations.

If the court finds discrimination, what remedies are available? The federal court may do any of several things. It may *enjoin*—that is, order the employer to stop doing certain acts—or order the employer to take some action, such as reinstating or upgrading the employee or providing retroactive pay increases. The court may also award damages and/or grant attorney fees to the winning party.

In one case, the judge awarded attorney fees to the government, thus requiring the employee who was not successful in proving discrimination to pay the government for the costs of defending the case. The court decided that the employee's claim was not made in good faith, finding that her lawsuit was "the culmination of a long series of intentionally vindictive and abusive actions taken to harass her supervisors."

Employees may also have a claim for equal pay under the federal Equal Pay Act, when the employer pays wages at a different rate than what it pays employees of the opposite sex. The work must be equal, requiring equal skill, effort, and responsibility.[40]

Federal law prohibits age discrimination unless it is reasonably necessary to the normal operation of the particular business.[41]

Problem 22

   A. Diane Rawlinson is refused employment as a correctional officer because she fails to meet the 120-pound weight and 5-foot-2-inch height requirements. Do you think Diane would win if she argued that she was discriminated against on the basis of her sex? What proof would be helpful to show the court in order to get a decision in her favor?

   B. In a state correctional institution, the Department of Corrections adopted a regulation that any correctional officer who wanted to be promoted to lieutenant had to pass a certain personality test. An Hispanic correctional officer is denied a promotion because he has not been able to pass such a test. If he is able to show that 3 percent of all Hispanic people pass this personality test while 40 percent of all nonminorities pass, does he have a valid discrimination claim? Upon what additional factor might your answer depend?

   C. The administrator of a jail for male inmates has hired male and female officers. In an attempt to provide for the inmates' right to privacy, the administrator has made selective work assignments so that females only work the guard tower and monitor the video screens at the control center. A male officer believes that the women have the easy jobs and that the men have all the difficult jobs. Does he have a valid claim of job discrimination?

EMPLOYEE UNIONS

Under the Constitution's freedom of association clause, employees in both the public and private sectors have the right to join or to refrain from joining unions. This right extends to law enforcement personnel and correctional officers, even if the organization advocates illegal strikes.[42]

Collective bargaining is a form of negotiation giving employees the opportunity to meet and set wages, hours, and other terms and conditions of employment with their employer. For it to be effective, both parties must deal with each other in an open and fair manner (in "good faith") with the goal of achieving a workable agreement. Some collective bargaining agreements call for outside *mediators* or *arbitrators.* In some cases, if both sides can't agree, an arbitrator will make a binding decision. Others do not allow binding agreements but rather have "meet and confer" arrangements. Though nongovernmental employees have a right to bargain collectively under the National Labor Relations Act, public employees must look to their state laws to determine if collective bargaining is permitted. As of 1983, 40 states and the District of Columbia had some type of public-sector collective bargaining laws, but only about one-third of state correctional agencies have signed collective bargaining agreements with one type of employee organization or another.

Unions and collective bargaining among correctional personnel are controversial issues, especially since corrections traditionally has been organized more on the military than the industrial model. Therefore, some believe unionization can undermine the necessary order, discipline, and control required for work in corrections. Others believe that correctional personnel should be able to bargain for higher wages, employee safety, benefits, and even a voice in decisions regarding inmate programs and prison policy. This last request by some corrections unions may raise particular problems, because it may diminish the power of corrections administrators or even the state legislature to make policy decisions for corrections and exercise what are termed "management rights."

Unless a state requires collective bargaining with unions or unless there is a collective bargaining agreement, correctional administrators and state officials are not required to recognize or deal with unions.

Correctional employees cannot be required to be members of unions, but if the state recognizes a union as the only bargaining agent for employees, the employees can be required to pay a service fee, for gains won in negotiations. Some corrections unions allow administrators and supervisors to join local unions along with correctional officers, while others do not. The courts are split as to whether restricting union membership in this way is legal. Therefore, state law will have to be checked on this issue. However, if higher-ranking officers are not allowed to join, they can form their own union.

A controversial issue involving unions is whether there should be a right to strike. In most states, public employees do not have this right and can be arrested for such action; law enforcement personnel are almost always specifically forbidden to strike.

Problem 23

Do you agree or disagree with the following statement: "Every state should have a law allowing unions and collective bargaining for correctional employees?"

A. What are the reasons for your opinion?

B. If correctional officers do unionize, can the union help them with the following complaints or problems? If so, how?

1. Assaults on officers

2. Officer coverage during inmate transfers

3. Wages

4. Life insurance

5. The number of positions to be filled by females

6. The number of civilian and noncivilian positions

7. Training programs and college benefits

8. Overtime pay

9. Uniform allowances

10. Grievance procedures

11. Inmate educational programs

C. Do you think a correctional officer union should share in decision making in the areas listed? Explain.

References

1. Davidson v. Dixon, 386 F.Supp. 482 (D.Del.1974), aff'd 529 F.2d 511 (3d Cir.1975).
2. Green v. Hawkins, U.S.Dist.Ct. (D.Md.1977).
3. ACA Correctional Law Project. See Appendix D.
4. Soto v. Dickey, 744 F.2d 1260 (7th Cir.1984), cert. denied 470 U.S. 1085, 105 S.Ct. 1846 (1985).

5. Slakan v. Porter, 737 F.2d 368 (4th Cir.1984), cert. denied sub nom. Reed v. Slakan, 470 U.S. 1035, 105 S.Ct. 1413 (1985).

6. 471 U.S. 1, 105 S.Ct. 1694 (1985).

7. Whitley v. Albers, 475 U.S. ___, 106 S.Ct. 1078 (1986).

8. Whitley v. Albers, Supra.

9. Marchese v. Lucas, 758 F.2d 181 (6th Cir.1985).

10. Anonymous v. District of Columbia, D.C.Sup.Ct. (1977).

11. 471 U.S. 808, 105 S.Ct. 2427 (1985).

12. Oklahoma City v. Tuttle, Supra.

13. Pembaur v. City of Cincinnati, 475 U.S. ___, 106 S.Ct. 1292 (1986).

14. Barnard v. State, 265 N.W.2d 620 (Iowa 1978).

15. Riley v. Jeffes, 777 F.2d 143 (3d Cir.1985).

16. Harris v. Chanclor, 537 F.2d 203 (5th Cir.1976).

17. Wiggins v. Sargent, 753 F.2d 663 (8th Cir.1985).

18. Daniels v. Andersen, 195 Neb. 95, 237 N.W.2d 397 (1975).

19. Porter v. County of Cook, 42 Ill.App.3d 287, 355 N.E.2d 561 (1976).

20. Blevins v. Brew, 593 F.Supp. 245 (W.D.Wis.1984).

21. Walker v. Interstate Fire and Casualty, 334 So.2d 714 (La.App.1976).

22. West v. Keve, 571 F.2d 158 (3d Cir.1978), further proceedings 541 F.Supp. 534 (D.Del.1982).

23. Robert Ellis Smith, *Privacy,* (New York: Anchor Press/Doubleday, 1979).

24. Jacobson v. Massachusetts, 197 U.S. 11, 25 S.Ct. 358 (1905), State ex rel. Holcolm v. Armstrong, 39 Wash.2d 860, 239 P.2d 545 (1952).

25. William Paul Isele, "Jail Inmate's Right to Refuse Medical Treatment," *Americans for Effective Law Enforcement,* Vol. 78–9:14.

26. Owens v. Alldridge, 311 F.Supp. 667 (W.D.Okl.1970).

27. In re Sanchez, 577 F.Supp. 7 (S.D.N.Y.1983).

28. Zant v. Prevatte, 248 Ga. 832, 286 S.E.2d 715 (Ga.Sup.Ct.1982).

29. Bee v. Greaves, 744 F.2d 1387 (10th Cir.1984), cert. denied 469 U.S. 1214, 105 S.Ct. 1187 (1985).

30. 42 U.S.C.A. § 3701.

31. Dothard v. Rawlinson, 433 U.S. 321, 97 S.Ct. 2720 (1977).

32. Forts v. Ward, 621 F.2d 1210 (2d Cir.1980).

33. Grummett v. Rushen, 779 F.2d 491 (9th Cir.1985).

34. Bagley v. Watson, 579 F.Supp. 1099 (D.Ore.1983).

35. Bagley v. Watson, Supra.

36. 29 CFR Section 1604.11(a).

37. 29 CFR Section 1604.11(d).

38. 29 CFR Section 1604.11(e).

39. Meritor Savings Bank v. Vinson, 477 U.S. ___, 106 S.Ct. 2399 (1986).

40. 29 U.S.C.A. § 206(d)(1).

41. 29 U.S.C.A. § 623.

42. Police Officers' Guild, National Association of Police Officers v. Washington, 369 F.Supp. 543 (D.D.C.1973).

CHAPTER 3

Prisoners' Rights

INTRODUCTION TO PRISONERS' RIGHTS

In discussing "rights" of prisoners in this chapter, we are generally referring to rights conferred by the U.S. Constitution. How the Constitution applies to jails and prisons has been determined principally by the Supreme Court and other federal courts. However, it should be remembered that state constitutions and other state and local laws, cases from state courts, and regulations of each individual Department of Corrections, prison, and/or jail also define such "rights." In some cases, local and state regulations have provided inmates with greater rights than the courts or the Constitution guarantee. Always check these regulations, because violations of rules or regulations can also form grounds for a lawsuit.

Problem 24

The Constitution gives certain fundamental rights to each citizen. These include freedom of speech, freedom from unreasonable searches and seizures, privacy, and freedom of association. When a person enters a jail or prison, these rights are limited by the needs and nature of the institution.

Give your reasons for and against limiting these rights in a correctional institution.

Generally, federal constitutional rights are more restricted in institutions than on the outside, but it is inaccurate to state that rights do not exist when a person is incarcerated. As now Supreme Court Justice Harry Blackmun said in one of his Circuit Court opinions: "Fundamental rights follow the prisoner through the walls which incarcerate him, but always with appropriate limitations."

In deciding how much a right should be limited, the courts often use what is called "the *balancing test.*" This means that the court balances the importance of protecting the individual's rights against the importance of restricting them. For example, in a free speech case, the courts look at the need for allowing an inmate to say something and weigh it against the danger to security in the institution if the speech is made. The courts will grant prison and jail administrators a great deal of latitude in deciding what limits are properly placed on inmates' rights. However, the courts will act to protect constitutional rights when the institutions have failed to provide the constitutional guarantees. Courts look for the following when an inmate complains of constitutional rights' violations:

- whether or not the activity is actually protected by the Constitution;
- what danger is involved in the institution (specific dangers that are backed up by specific explanations of the connection between the alleged danger and the activity);
- what governmental interest is at stake; and
- whether the governmental interest at stake is a proper one for the particular institution involved.

The court will then balance the right of the inmate with the government's interest.

RIGHTS OF PRETRIAL DETAINEES

A further development in inmate rights is the issue of whether those who are in jail awaiting trial but who have not yet been convicted (called *pretrial detainees*) should be provided greater rights than those who have already been convicted.

Why should pretrial detainees have greater rights? The answer sometimes given is that these inmates are still presumed innocent and are in jail only to ensure their appearance in court, not to be punished or rehabilitated. The courts have acknowledged that making sure the defendant appears at trial requires that jails be secure and well managed. Most pretrial detainees are in jail solely because they could not produce the money *bond* placed on them. If they had the money, most pretrial

detainees would be on the street, enjoying the much fuller protection of the Constitution accorded to ordinary citizens.

In the past, the constitutional rights of prisoners have been restricted due to the prison's interest in security, order, rehabilitation, and punishment. Until 1979, most prisoners' rights cases had been applied to jails and prisons without drawing a distinction between them.

In *Bell v. Wolfish,* the U.S. Supreme Court decided that restrictions on the rights of pretrial detainees will be judged for their constitutionality under a "punishment" test.[1] The court ruled that the due process clause

179

of the Fifth Amendment to the Constitution prohibits restrictions on
pretrial detainees that amount to punishment. "A convicted inmate, on
the other hand, may be punished, although that punishment may not be
'cruel and unusual' under the Eighth Amendment." [2]

In 1981, the Supreme Court, in *Rhodes v. Chapman,* defined cruel and
unusual punishment when it ruled that the Eighth Amendment prohibits punishments that, although not physically barbarous, involve the
unnecessary and wanton infliction of pain or that are grossly disproportionate to the severity of the crime warranting imprisonment.[3] Punishments involving the unnecessary and wanton infliction of pain are
totally without penological justification.

In applying this standard in *Rhodes* to double-celling of convicted
inmates in an otherwise "top-flight" facility, the Court said that conditions were constitutional. To the extent that such conditions are restrictive or even harsh, the Court held they are part of the penalty that
criminal offenders pay for their offenses against society.

It is often difficult for jail personnel to decide what amounts to
appropriate punishment for pretrial detainees. In *Bell v. Wolfish,* the
Supreme Court listed the following factors as guideposts in determining
whether actions by officials are punishment of pretrial detainees.[4]

- ◆ Whether the action involves an affirmative disability or restraint;
- ◆ Whether historically the action was regarded as punishment;
- ◆ Whether the action comes into play only on a finding of knowl-
  edge;
- ◆ Whether the action will promote the traditional aims of punish-
  ment—retribution and deterrence;
- ◆ Whether there is another rational purpose for the action besides
  punishment; or
- ◆ Whether this other purpose for the restriction is excessive.

In summary, the Supreme Court said that actions will constitute
punishment: (1) if there is an expressed intent on the part of correctional officials to punish; (2) if there is no rational connection between the
rule or restriction and the purpose for the rule other than punishment
(e.g., security, internal order, and discipline reasons); or (3) where that
other purpose is excessive in relation to the nonpunitive reason given
for the rule.

In 1984 in *Block v. Rutherford,* the Supreme Court again took the opportunity to discuss the rights of pretrial detainees when it decided that
denial of contact visits did not amount to punishment. The Supreme
Court applied the three criteria of punishment and found that the
officials' intent was not to punish. Instead, the purpose was to provide

security within the jail, and a ban on contact visits was found to be rationally related to the internal security needs of a jail.[5]

In examining the security requirements of a jail, the Court said:

> "Detainees—by definition persons unable to meet bail—often are awaiting trial for serious, violent offenses, and many have prior criminal convictions. It is no answer, of course, that we deal here with restrictions on pretrial detainees rather than convicted criminals. For, in this context, there is no basis for concluding that pretrial detainees pose any lesser security risk than convicted inmates. Indeed, it may be that in certain circumstances detainees present a greater risk to jail security and order."

The Supreme Court found that a total ban on contact visits was neither excessive nor arbitrary. Additionally, the Court was unwilling to substitute its judgment on the difficult and sensitive matters of institutional administration and security for that of the persons who are charged with and trained in running the institutions.[6]

Problem 25

Should pretrial detainees be provided different rights than convicted inmates? Why or why not?

One new question on prisoner rights arises because of the development of "private prisons." Private contractors have entered the prison and jail market, offering to provide everything from individual services such as medical care to operating the entire institution. In one case involving a private security firm that was running a federal facility to detain illegal aliens, a federal judge ruled that the government was still liable for unconstitutional actions taken by the private contractor. The court said that, because the power to detain is a government function, any arrangements made to detain inmates brought into play all the constitutional protections to which they were entitled.[7]

RIGHTS TO FREEDOM OF SPEECH, RELIGION, ASSOCIATION, AND THE PRESS

The First Amendment: *"Congress shall make no law respecting an establishment of religion, or prohibiting the free exercise thereof; or abridging the freedom of speech, or of the press; or the right of the people peaceably to assemble, and to petition the Government for a redress of grievances."*

Freedom of Speech

Speech can be defined as the communication of thoughts and ideas. This may include an inmate talking to another inmate, writing a letter to a friend, publishing a newsletter, or wearing an armband as a symbolic act.

Many dangers to and interests of correctional institutions are involved in limiting the various activities protected by the First Amendment. For example:

Activity	Danger	Government Interest in Limiting Activity
Talking to another inmate	Make escape plans, plan other crimes, create riot or disturbance	Security, order, rehabilitation
Sending mail to friend	Escape plan, contact with negative influences, unauthorized entry by others	Security, rehabilitation
Receiving mail from persons with attorney address	Imposter sending escape plans, *contraband,* too much mail	Security, rehabilitation, administrative convenience

In trying to determine when free speech under the First Amendment can be restricted, the U.S. Supreme Court has used a number of different tests. In one of the oldest, called the clear and present danger test, the Court looks at the circumstances under which the words were used and decides whether the speech would create a "clear and present danger" of causing harm to another person or society.

Another test in free speech cases is the balancing test: The Court looks at the circumstances involved and attempts to balance the interests of society against the interests of the individual in expressing his or her ideas.

The Supreme Court set the general standard for reviewing First Amendment cases in the case of *Procunier v. Martinez:* The regulation of free speech in prison must further an important or substantial government issue unrelated to the suppression of free speech, and the restriction must be no greater than necessary to protect that interest.[8]

There are also certain types of speech that are not protected by the First Amendment. For example, a person's speech may not be expressed in a manner that will incite others to riot or to be violent. The speech cannot be obscene. According to the Supreme Court, speech is obscene when, taken as a whole by an average person applying contemporary community standards, it appeals to a prurient (lewd) interest in sex;

portrays sexual conduct in a patently obvious way; and lacks serious literary, artistic, political, or scientific value. Nor can it be "threatening to the point of causing an immediate disruption"—or what the court has called "fighting words." Moreover, the speech cannot be slanderous (false statements that damage another's reputation).

The Case of Procunier v. Martinez

In a 1974 Supreme Court case, inmates complained that California prison rules on mail violated their First Amendment rights. These rules prohibited sending letters that "unduly complain" or "magnify grievances," express "inflammatory political, racial, or religious or other views" or "pertain to criminal activity." They also banned letters which "are lewd, obscene, or defamatory; contain foreign matter; or are otherwise inappropriate."

Correctional officials claimed that censorship of inmate mail that "magnified grievances or unduly complained" was a precaution against the danger of riots and furthered inmate rehabilitation. However, correctional officials could not explain how outgoing mail containing such statements could lead to riots or could harm inmate rehabilitation. The Court went on to find that these rules did not further legitimate institutional interests of security, rehabilitation, or the preservation of internal order and discipline but were overbroad and vague and had as their sole purpose the suppression of expression and were, therefore, invalid.[9]

Courts also consider to whom the mail is being sent in determining the kinds of restrictions that will be enforced. Courts agree that mail to and from lawyers and courts should not be censored. The Sixth Amendment right of access to *counsel* and the courts, as well as the First Amendment right of free speech, apply to this category of mail.

In *Wolff v. McDonnell*, a 1974 Supreme Court case, the Court said that mail to convicted inmates, even from an attorney, could be opened to inspect for contraband. The court went on to say that attorney mail should only be opened in the inmates' presence because officials would then be less likely to read the mail.[10]

Lower courts have examined specific mail regulations and the institution's reasons for them and sometimes have ruled that they violated the First Amendment. For example, in one case, little or no restriction was allowed regarding mail to the news media.[11]

In another case, a court ruled as valid a prison policy restricting mail to inmates in temporary disciplinary confinement so they could only receive first-class mail of a personal, legal, or religious nature. The court said this furthered the important government issue of making disciplinary detention unattractive to inmates. Other reasons that were found to be insufficient to justify the policy were to prevent cellblock fires or to make cell searches easier.[12] A court has struck down rules that required officials to approve names on an inmate's mailing list and restricted the number of persons on the list and the overall number of

letters sent. This same court required that postage be provided an indigent inmate for letters to attorneys and the media and five others per week.[13]

On the other hand, one federal court ruled that a prison's policy of refusing to pay postage for legal mail when an inmate is able to provide postage for his personal mail did not violate the Constitution.[14] A federal court of appeals ruled that the one prison rule limiting indigent inmates to two free twenty-cent stamps a week for legal correspondence was reasonable. The court noted that the inmate complaining of the policy presented no evidence that any of his lawsuits were dismissed or that any sanction was imposed by the courts due to the stamp policy.[15]

Another question regarding free speech is the censorship of publications that can be received by or distributed to inmates. One district court allowed the distribution of *Fortune News,* which is published by the Fortune Society "to create public awareness of the prison systems." The court said the prison officials needed to show a "compelling state interest" to justify banning the newsletter or a "clear and present danger to prison discipline or security." Other courts, however, have only required officials to show that the censored material would have a detrimental effect on a legitimate government interest.[16]

In *Bell v. Wolfish,* the U.S. Supreme Court also upheld a "publisher only" rule for pretrial detainees who spent a maximum of sixty days in jail. This rule allowed correctional officials, who were concerned about serious security and administrative problems, to require that hardcover books be received by inmates only when they were mailed directly from bookstores, publishers, and book clubs.[17]

Problem 26

Does your First Amendment right to free speech protect you under the following circumstances?

A. You call your friend on the telephone and say you think the President is a bum. Can you be convicted of a crime for this? What if you stand on a park bench and do this? What if you block an intersection and do it?

B. You keep a diary at home and write that the city government is racist and should be overthrown. What if you said the same things to a crowd on a street corner or on television? Can you be arrested?

C. You wear a black arm band to school signifying your protest of a war, and arguments take place. Can you be suspended or expelled?

D. You receive at home a communist publication that calls for the overthrow of all capitalist countries. Can the government stop this or arrest you?

Problem 27 ♦ Freedom of Speech Role-play

Martin Sostre, while an inmate in Green Haven Prison in New York, violated prison rules and was placed in solitary confinement. Shortly after his release, he was deprived of the use of the prison exercise yard and the privilege of attending movies because he had "inflammatory racial literature" in his cell. The literature consisted of articles written by Sostre on paper properly in his possession. Most of the articles were extracts from magazines and newsletters Sostre was permitted to have in his cell. The literature included quotations from Mao Tse Tung; poetry of another inmate; the names of officers and the party program and rules of conduct of the Black Panther Party; officers and the oath of allegiance of the Republic of New Africa; the poem "If We Must Die" by Claude McKay; and an article Sostre wrote titled "Revolutionary Thoughts."

   A. Was the punishment imposed on Sostre for putting his thoughts on paper a violation of his First Amendment rights?

   B. Should he have been able to keep his writings?

   C. Can Sostre distribute them to other inmates?

Sostre had initially filed a Section 1983 Civil Rights claim alleging that the warden's actions in punishing him for his writings violated his First Amendment rights. This situation should be role-played as a *mock* hearing of legal arguments at a trial. Those playing attorneys should base their arguments on the preceding facts and the law described in this section. Both sides agree to these facts.

A panel of three judges is needed to hear the arguments, to question the attorneys, and to decide (majority wins) which position is correct on each of the three questions. Two attorneys will represent and argue the state's position on each of these three questions, and two attorneys will argue the inmate's position.

Problem 28

Discuss whether an inmate's First Amendment rights are violated in the following situations.

   A. Can an inmate be stopped from verbally criticizing the way a jail is run? Does it make a difference if he or she actively seeks out other inmates to discuss this topic?

   B. A prison has a rule forbidding the possession of obscene materials. An inmate has a copy of what Officer Dean considers to be an obscene homosexually oriented magazine. Can the officer take it away? Can the officer take *Playboy* or *Hustler* away?

   C. A convicted inmate is reading a letter from the outside. Can correctional personnel in the institution take it and read it, or can they censor it before the inmate receives it?

Freedom of Religion

The First Amendment prevents the government from either establishing religion or restricting its free exercise. Therefore, the state cannot tell people what church to go to ("establishment") or tell them they cannot go to church at all ("restricting free exercise"). As the Supreme Court has said, there is supposed to be a "wall of separation between church and state" in our country.

Freedom of religion may sometimes be restricted outside correctional institutions, as when it conflicts with a serious governmental interest. For example, the Mormon religion allowed men to have more than one wife, and state law made this a crime. The U.S. Supreme Court ruled such marriages could be outlawed because the government's interest in preserving the American family was more important than allowing this religious practice.

Religious belief or thought cannot be restricted in a correctional institution, but religious practice may be curtailed when it affects discipline or security within the institution. If restrictions are overbroad or lacking in substance, they are unconstitutional.

During the 1960s, many cases were brought by Black Muslims concerning their right to practice religion in prison. Recent decisions have held that Black Muslims should be permitted to have congregational services, a minister, and religious literature. The courts have generally said that prison officials should create rules and regulations that, as much as possible, permit religious groups what they want, provided prison security is protected.

An interesting case arose in a federal prison where a group of inmates organized their own religion and called it The Church of the New Song. A court held that prison officials must allow this if it was really a religious group and not a cover-up for some other purpose.[18] In deciding what constitutes a true religion, courts apply standards pertaining to the group's history, age, whether it has characteristics similar to other religions, and how sincere the followers appear to be.

This Church of the New Song has subsequently spread to other prisons. A federal district court in Texas found that, despite a belief in a supreme being, the political and nonreligious tone of its services showed that the church was not a religion but, rather, a masquerade designed to obtain First Amendment protection for acts that would otherwise be unlawful in prison. The court said that, even if it were a religion, prison officials would have the right to deny an inmate's demand to have all the rights of a prison chaplain. This "chaplain" inmate was classified as an escape artist and dangerous felon. The right to exercise religion can be restricted by a compelling state interest—here, the maintenance of prison discipline.[19]

Courts differ on how much religious practice may be restricted. In one case, the court said that it was permissible to forbid dangerous prisoners from attending religious services.[20]

Institutional rules that forbid beards and long hair, though generally upheld by courts, have in some cases been ruled unconstitutional on religious grounds. For example, in one case, a Native American was allowed to have long hair as his religion required.[21] In 1978, Congress passed the American Indian Religious Freedom Act, which makes it an express federal policy to protect the religious freedom of Native American people.[22] This act makes it more difficult to restrict Indian religious practices, at least within federal prisons.

One area of contention has been religious diets. Some courts have held that a prison need not provide special religious dietary foods, particularly where prison policies provide inmates with nutritionally adequate diets by substituting more of one menu item for the prohibited food.[23]

However, similar cases brought by jail inmates have found the courts more obliging to requests for religious diets. One court required reduced use of pork in meal preparation at a jail to allow a Black Muslim a pork-free diet. In *Miller v. Carson,* a federal court of appeals found that restrictions on the religious activities of pretrial detainees in a Florida jail violated the freedom of religion clause. Inmates were not provided any special dietary considerations, and, because the sheriff raised hogs, pork was served or used as a seasoning in all meals.[24]

In a Michigan jail, pretrial detainees with bonds of $5,000 or more were not allowed to attend chapel, while those with less than $5,000 bonds were allowed to attend. The federal district court found this restriction to be arbitrary and a denial of the right of free exercise of religion.[25]

Another freedom of religion issue occurs when inmates are transferred as a penalty for their religious beliefs. A California court held this a violation of the First Amendment.[26]

Problem 29

Are a person's First Amendment rights violated in the following situations?

   A. Do two Hanafi Muslim prison inmates have a constitutional right to keep their white, full-length, hooded robes in their cells, since they wish to wear them at least five times a day during their prayers? Prison officials want to restrict use of the robes to the prison chapel because of a prior incident in which an officer used a robe to frighten an inmate into believing a Ku Klux Klan member was chasing him and because the robes could be used to conceal contraband and be modified to civilian dress to aid in escape.

B. May prison officials constitutionally ban inmates affiliated with a Christian church that ministers to the religious and spiritual needs of homosexuals from participating in group worship services? Other churches are permitted to hold group worship services. Prison officials have evidence indicating a strong correlation between inmate homosexuality and prison violence, including at least twenty-six incidents of serious violence, three of which were homicides.

C. A Buddhist inmate wants to use the chapel and write a letter to his religious advisor. Can he be prevented from doing so? If an institution pays for Catholic and Protestant chaplains, must it also hire a Buddhist one?

D. A prison has a rule against wearing medals of any kind. Can a Muslim inmate wear a religious medal?

E. An inmate who has been placed in segregation wants to go to the chapel. Can he be prevented from doing so?

Problem 30

Are there any benefits to the institution or society if inmates are allowed to practice their religion in an institution? If yes, list them.

Problem 31

Five inmates get together and declare themselves to be the Church of the New Faith. They say prayers to their God and establish ten pages of rules they must follow. Decide if each of the following items they request must be provided:

A. their own paid chaplain because the institution pays for a Catholic and a Protestant chaplain;

B. pizza to have as communion in their services;

C. the right to use the chapel for a service on Sunday just as other religions do;

D. an optional service for the entire prison population of 500 in the yard;

E. the right to circulate their rules to members;

F. complete privacy from staff during their services.

Freedom of Association: Visitation and Prisoner Unions

Visitation   Restrictions on inmate visitation are discussed in the context of the First Amendment's freedom of association, due process' ban on punishment of pretrial detainees, or under the prohibition of cruel and unusual punishment.[27] Whether visitation by family and friends is a right or a privilege has not yet been decided by the Supreme Court.

Several federal courts have found that visitation for pretrial detainees is a right. The U.S. Supreme Court has made it clear that contact visitation is not a right of pretrial detainees.[28]

Although it is not exactly clear how much visitation must be provided to inmates or pretrial detainees, the following rules have been struck down as too restrictive:

1. A regulation permitting a pretrial detainee one visit with family members for no more than fifteen minutes a week.[29]
2. A regulation allowing inmates one visit during the week with two of five persons on the inmate's approved list.[30]

Lawsuits demanding *conjugal visits* (permitting sexual relations) as a right have not been successful, and very few institutions allow this. Community opposition to conjugal visits and the possible resulting conception of children who would often be added to welfare roles is the primary reason given for not allowing them.

Privacy during visitation has been raised in a number of cases, but the courts have always ruled that inmates have no absolute right to privacy. The one instance where inmates appear to have the right not to have their conversations monitored by correctional personnel is attorney visits. Of course, attorney visits may be visually monitored for the safety of the attorney.

Monitoring inmates' phone calls by use of an extension phone or other device may violate federal and/or state law. In one recent case, the federal law protecting people against willful interception of telephone calls was applied to correctional officials' eavesdropping on an inmate's phone call.[31] The inmate had not been notified that calls were monitored, and no departmental regulations permitted it. The usual procedure for monitoring calls in this prison was for an officer to be stationed near enough the phone to hear the conversation. A single incident of eavesdropping through a phone extension was held to violate an inmate's right to privacy and correctional officials were required to pay damages of $100 for each day of the violation or $1,000, whichever was greater; punitive damages; and reasonable attorney's fees.[32]

Due process requires that regulations limiting visitation be clear and not applied in an arbitrary way. Additionally, the *equal protection* clause forbids prison officials from differentiating between inmates on the basis of race, religion, or other unlawful criteria.

Prisoners' Unions   Can a prison legally enact rules to prohibit inmates from soliciting other inmates to join a union, to *bar* all union meetings, and to refuse to deliver packets of union publications that had been mailed to several inmates for distribution to other inmates? The following facts are from a 1977 Supreme Court case.

The Case of Jones v. North Carolina Prisoners' Labor Union

Inmates in a state prison, claiming that the First and Fourteenth Amendment rights of the union and of its members were being violated, filed a Section 1983 lawsuit (see p. 145). The state's position was that, while it allowed inmates to be members of the union, for reasons of security and the orderly functioning of the institution, it did not allow solicitation (asking inmates to become new members), union meetings (although other groups were allowed to meet, e.g., Alcoholics Anonymous and the Jaycees), or bulk mailings to inmates. The Supreme Court upheld the prison limits on these union activities, leaving it up to correctional officials to determine the dangers involved.

The Court found that solicitation of members involved more than the simple expression of views but was an invitation to engage collectively in an activity that could be prohibited. The Court found that freedom of association could be restricted in view of reasonable considerations of penal management. In regard to the argument that other groups were allowed to solicit members and make mailings, the Court required that the corrections department show only a rational basis for distinguishing between its treatment of such groups as Alcoholics Anonymous and the Jaycees and the inmate union. The rational basis accepted by the court was that the former groups, which were allowed to meet, worked in harmony with the institution, while the union posed a threat to security. Likewise, a restriction on bulk mailings did not violate freedom of speech, since other means of providing outside information were available to the union.[33]

Problem 32

A state prison inmate claimed he had a right to wear a button showing a picture of a barred window or door and the words "Prison Union." The state Department of Corrections did not permit unions to solicit or have meetings in the prison.

   A. Does wearing the union button constitute "speech" protected by the Constitution?

   B. Can the prison legitimately prohibit wearing the button? Why or why not?

Freedom of the Press

Two issues regarding freedom of the press are: (1) an inmate's right to publish a newsletter or a manuscript, and (2) the right of the press to interview inmates.

Many institutions have rules stating that inmates may not publish materials without the approval of correctional officials. Institutions have justified these rules for reasons of security—for example, that obscene materials are harmful, that criminal histories promote crime—or for reasons of justice—for example, that criminals should not profit from their wrongdoing. Though only a few cases have challenged such rules, they usually have been ruled constitutional.[34] However, many institutions allow inmates to write or publish freely, and some states have even passed laws guaranteeing inmates the right to own their own writings.

Other states (for example, Ohio) have passed laws disallowing profit from criminal life stories and require putting money made into restitution funds for victims of crime. The impetus for these statutes are cases of notorious prisoners earning large royalties from books, movies, and so on.

In regard to the right to be interviewed by the press, the U.S. Supreme Court has ruled that no such right exists and that prisons may restrict access to the press.[35] Because the press, through other regulations, had access to prisons, could inspect all conditions, conduct brief

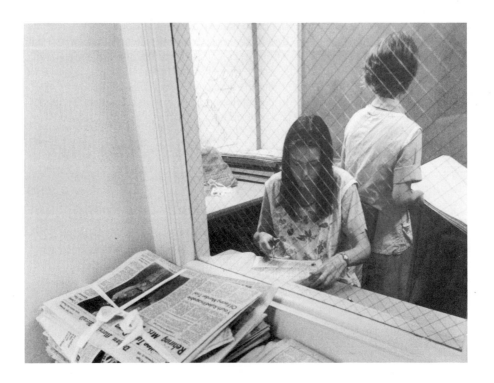

interviews with inmates, and interview recently released inmates, the Court upheld regulations giving newspersons the same restricted right to the prison as the general public. The general rule was that only inmates' families, attorneys, and religious counsel had a right to visit inmates.

A local television station reported on a suicide in a California jail and included a statement by the institution's psychiatrist that the conditions of the facility were responsible for his patient-prisoner's suicide, as well as a statement by the sheriff denying that this was the case. The station then requested permission from the sheriff to inspect and take pictures of the jail. After permission was denied, the station filed a Section 1983 lawsuit to gain access at reasonable times, to use cameras and recorders, and to interview inmates. The station based its claim on the First Amendment right of freedom of the press. While the suit was pending, the sheriff established a program of regular monthly tours, but the tours did not include the facility where the suicide had occurred. Although pictures of some areas were provided, no cameras or tape recorders were permitted on the tour. No interviews of inmates were allowed, and inmates were generally out of sight.

The station claimed that, under the press's constitutional right to gather news and information, it had an implied special right of access to government-controlled information. Access to penal institutions was argued as necessary to prevent officials from concealing conditions from the voters and impairing the public's right to discuss and criticize the correctional system and administration.

The sheriff said his reasons for limiting access by the press were that: (1) unregulated access by the media would infringe on inmate privacy; (2) interviews tend to create "jail celebrities," who in turn often generate internal problems and undermine jail security; and (3) unscheduled tours could disrupt jail operations.

The sheriff outlined the alternatives by which jail information could reach the public: mail, visits by news reporters to inmates whom they personally knew, and phone contact by social service workers to help inmates with problems.

The U.S. Supreme Court agreed with the sheriff's finding that the First Amendment did not give the news media the right of access to government information or sources of information beyond that available to the public generally.[36]

Problem 33

In the following situations, what, if any, First Amendment rights are involved?

   A. You believe the police are unduly harassing citizens who drive cars at night in your neighborhood. Can you publish a newsletter criticizing the police and distribute it to all your neighbors? Can you call up the local newspaper and talk to a reporter about it?

   B. Inmates wish to publish a newspaper criticizing prison policies and to list officials by name. Can the prison forbid such a publication?

C. An inmate writes a letter to a newspaper and tells about jail conditions. Can the paper interview him?

SEARCHES AND PRIVACY ISSUES

The Fourth Amendment: *"The right of the people to be secure in their persons, houses, papers, and effects, against unreasonable searches and seizures, shall not be violated, and no warrants shall issue, but upon probable cause, supported by oath or affirmation, and particularly describing the place to be searched, and the persons or things to be seized."*

The Fourth Amendment outlaws unreasonable searches by the government of areas where there is a legitimate expectation of privacy. The word "legitimate" is key here because the concept of legitimacy is tested by what *society,* not the individual, believes to be private.

Many states also have state constitutional rights or statutes that regulate governmental searches. Correctional agencies, out of necessity, have often adopted detailed rules and procedures governing searches of inmates, employees, and visitors. For the most part, courts have given correctional officials broad rights to search inmates and their personal belongings, and no search warrant has been required. Some recent cases, however, have pointed out that inmates have the right to be free from arbitrary, harassing, or unnecessary searches.

Two questions that often arise in this area are: (1) Does an inmate have a reasonable expectation of privacy in the area or part of the body searched, and (2) if so, was the specific search "reasonable"?

Do inmates have a legitimate expectation of privacy to their belongings in their cells? Clearly, most inmates believe that they expect the items they store in their cells to be kept private. However, the U.S. Supreme Court ruled in *Hudson v. Palmer* that there is no legitimate expectation of privacy in an inmate's papers and property in a cell.[37] The Court ruled that society is not willing to provide this type of privacy protection, since privacy in cells is "fundamentally incompatible with the close and continual surveillance of inmates and their cells required to insure institutional security and internal order."

Since inmates have no legitimate expectation of privacy in the search and seizure of items in their cells, it is unnecessary to ask the next question—"Is the cell search reasonable?"

The Supreme Court did say, however, that the absence of Fourth Amendment protections did not mean that correctional officers could run roughshod over an inmate's property rights. If searches are conducted solely to harass inmates, they still would be protected by the cruel and unusual punishment clause. If personal property was destroyed, the inmates still would have a right to file a tort suit in state court to recover damages from the officer.

In the same case, the Supreme Court also made it clear that the inmates do not have the right to be present during cell searches.

Society is willing to provide greater protection to the privacy of an inmate's body. In legal terms, inmates have a legitimate expectation of privacy in their bodies. Government searches of inmate bodies may, therefore, be conducted only if they are "reasonable."

In *Bell v. Wolfish,* the U.S. Supreme Court stated that, to determine the reasonableness of any specific search, courts should balance the need for the search against the invasion of privacy the search entails. In particular, the court instructed judges to consider:

1. the scope of a particular instrusion;
2. the manner in which it is conducted;
3. the justification for initiating the search; and
4. the place where it is conducted.[38]

The three primary types of searches of an inmate's body that occur in a jail or prison are a pat-down search, a strip search, and a body-cavity search.

Although agencies differ on how they define these searches, for the purposes of this discussion these definitions apply:

- ◆ Pat-down, or frisk, searches—Inspections of fully clothed persons using the hands, including the search of the inmate's clothing and personal effects. This could include having inmates remove objects from their pockets and subject themselves to a metal detector.

- ◆ Strip searches—Visual inspections of all body surfaces and all body cavities by correctional staff. Inmates are not touched by security personnel at any time during a search, but male inmates can be required to lift their genitals and bend over to spread their buttocks for visual inspection. Female inmates can be required to move in such a way to allow visual inspection of the vaginal and anal cavities.

- ◆ Body-cavity searches—Inspections for contraband in the anal and genital cavities by use of fingers or simple instruments. They should always be performed by medical staff.

Pat-down searches of inmates on a routine and/or random basis to control contraband are reasonable. If a particular inmate was singled out and searched once an hour, every hour, for days on end, a pat-down search could be unreasonable, unless, of course, there was sufficient justification for this treatment. (See chapter 2 for an examination of the conflict of this privacy right with the employment rights of staff.)

As the type of search becomes more intrusive—for example, a strip search—the question of what is reasonable and what is unreasonable becomes more troublesome.

Local law should be checked extremely carefully in this area, since the law and practices vary widely. However, the emerging rules on strip searches seem to be the following.

1. Strip searches of inmates in the general population can be done routinely after exposure to a significant opportunity to receive contraband—for instance, after contact visits, unsupervised furlough, court appearances, and work-release absences.

2. Routine searches of the entire institution or a portion of it may include strip searches of all inmates.

3. Strip searches at booking cannot be done routinely of all inmates. Persons arrested for minor misdemeanor and infraction offenses prior to arraignment who will be released in a few hours cannot be strip searched, unless there is sufficient justification, called a "reasonable belief," that a particular inmate is concealing a weapon or contraband. However, inmates being admitted to the general population of the jail may be strip searched.

In 1984, the U.S. Supreme Court refused to hear the case of *Giles v. Ackerman*.[39] This left standing the decision of the Circuit Court of Appeals that held that the Idaho police practice of requiring all arrestees to be strip searched and to have their body cavities visually inspected violated the Fourth Amendment. To justify a strip search of arrestees charged with minor offenses, jail officers must have a reasonable suspicion that the individual is carrying contraband, based on factors such as the nature of the charge and the arrestee's prior record and demeanor. Furthermore, there must be some indication that strip searches effectively deter smuggling of contraband into the facility. Here, the court ruled where arrest and confinement are unplanned, the policy of strip searching everyone could not possibly deter arrestees from carrying contraband.

Some states have gone so far as to make it a criminal misdemeanor to conduct a strip search at the booking of certain arrested persons who do not enter the general jail population.[40]

4. If none of the preceding situations applies, strip searches of individual inmates in the general population can only be conducted when there is a "reasonable belief" that a particular inmate is hiding some item.

The requirement of reasonable belief to conduct a search makes it crucial that officers document the factors observed that led the officer to have a reasonable belief the inmate was concealing contraband. Several suits have awarded compensatory and punitive damages to inmates being subjected to strip searches in violation of the Fourth Amendment.[41]

Remember, searches must always be conducted in a reasonable manner to ensure as much privacy as possible, with respect afforded the inmate. They must also be conducted by officers of the same sex unless this is absolutely impossible. If opposite-sex strip searches must be conducted, reasons must be fully documented.

The U.S. Supreme Court has stated that conducting strip searches in an abusive fashion will not be condoned.[42]

Urine testing for drugs raises questions of the constitutionality of this type of search and seizure. One federal court likened the urine tests to body-cavity searches, requiring the same level of judicial scrutiny.[43] In that case, the federal court said that a truly random process for selecting inmates for urine testing is constitutional.

Obviously, a body-cavity search involves an even greater intrusion and, as one court has said, should only be conducted when there is a "clear indication that the inmate is hiding contraband in a body cavity." A greasy substance found around the anus during a strip search

or an object partially viewed during a visual strip search are clear indications.

In every case, however, such a search should be conducted only by medical personnel and then only after approval by the top administrator or designee. It is essential that staff document the factors that led them to conduct such a search.

Are the rules for searches of staff and visitors the same as those for inmates? Should they be?

A prime requirement that must be met before any searches of visitors or employees may be conducted is that a notice must be posted that each person is subject to routine searches upon entering or leaving the grounds of the institution. This may be done in several ways, most simply by posting signs at all entrances that state: "All persons entering these grounds are subject to routine searches of their person, property, and packages." This notice permits routine frisk or pat searches of staff and visitors. However, it is fairly clear that courts will require at least as great a justification for a strip or body search of a visitor or employee as they would require for such searches of inmates.

In one case, the Court ruled that prison administrators may order a warrantless strip search of an officer if they have a reasonable suspicion that the officer is involved in smuggling contraband to inmates. However, to conduct the more intrusive visual body-cavity searches, administrators were required to get a judicially issued search warrant. Random, warrantless strip searches and visual body-cavity searches of employees were illegal.[44]

Problem 34

Inmates in one prison are selected for urine testing to detect marijuana in the following manner. The watch commander chooses the particular inmates by picking cards from a board in his office. This board holds a group of cards, each of which lists the name of an inmate. All inmates are represented on the board. Does this procedure violate the ban on unreasonable searches and seizures? NO - random

---

Problem 35 ◆ Hypotheticals on Strip Searches

Decide whether or not a strip search can be conducted on inmates in each of the following situations by applying the rules discussed in the text.

   A. Correctional officer walks by inmate's cell and sees inmate who quickly sits down. NO

B. Correctional officer observes inmate whose speech is slurred as if she were holding something in her mouth.   *yes*

C. Correctional officer observes an inmate pressing her arm to her side in an unusual manner.   *Yes*

D. Correctional officer observes an inmate walking in an unusual manner, suggesting she is hiding something in a body cavity. *yes*

E. A man is sitting in a jail lobby following his arrest for speeding and violating a restriction on his driver's license.   *No*

F. A correctional officer is told by an informant, who has given good information in the past, that Inmate Terry in cell #56 has contraband hidden on her person. The officer walks by cell #56 and sees Inmate Terry sit down quickly.   *yes*

G. When inmates are transferred from one county facility to another, they are strip searched at the facility from which they are being transferred. May they be strip searched at the receiving facility?

H. Inmates have contact visits. May they be strip searched after each contact visit?   *Yes*

I. Inmates have noncontact visits. May they be strip searched after each noncontact visit?   *No*

J. Inmates are allowed contact visits with attorneys. May officers conduct strip searches of inmates after attorney visits?   *No?*

K. Upon leaving the facility for unsupervised leave (temporary release, furlough, work release), may inmates be strip searched?   *Yes*

L. When an inmate is leaving on a supervised outside trip, may an officer strip search the inmate?   *No*

M. May strip searches be conducted as part of a general search of a facility or portion thereof?   *Yes*

N. Must the medical provider in the psychiatric housing area be of the same sex as the inmate in order to perform a strip search? *yes*

O. In conducting a routine strip search, how many officers may be present?

P. May multiple strip searches be conducted at the same time? If so, in what manner?

Related to searches is the issue of whether inmates have a right to return of confiscated items. Clearly, there is no right to the return of illegal items, such as weapons or drugs. However, courts have held that a receipt should be issued for legitimate items the inmate owns (e.g., books, clothes, jewelry), and these items should be returned when the inmate leaves the institution. Inmates have won money damages for lost items. In a 1985 study of lawsuits filed over two years by state and federal prison systems, the types of cases most frequently lost by corrections and most frequently settled by corrections were property claims.[45]

State statutes or rules that require depositing contraband money confiscated from an inmate into a general inmate welfare fund have been repeatedly upheld by courts.[46]

The right to privacy has also been raised in other circumstances involving correctional institutions. Cutting inmates' hair has been allowed by some courts for purposes of discipline, rehabilitation, security (in being able to identify inmates), and health reasons. Some cases, however, have restricted this practice.

Personnel at the Baltimore city jail, which has no standards for hair style or length, cut the hair of several inmates. The officials stated that long hair invited "deviate sexual advances and created hygienic problems." In finding that there were no health-care or identification problems within the jail with regard to the style or length of inmates' hair, the Court said that the jail should have a definite and reasonable policy if it finds it necessary to cut long hair. The Court also distinguished between pretrial and post-trial detainees, finding that it was constitutional to require convicted prisoners to conform to definite and reasonable hair regulations. But, the Court noted that it is not necessary to cut the hair of pretrial detainees.[47]

Some courts have also found it improper to cut an inmate's hair as punishment, and damages have even been awarded in some such cases. In recent years, many institutions have liberalized rules regulating hair length and facial hair.

ACCESS TO THE COURTS, ACCESS TO ATTORNEYS

These two rights involve inmates' ability to communicate with a lawyer or a court, to receive legal assistance from others, and to obtain legal materials to work on their cases by themselves. (See the Free Speech section of this chapter on p. 78 for a more extensive discussion of inmates' rights to mail letters to attorneys and courts.)

In one of the early "access to the court" cases decided by the Supreme Court, it was held improper for prison officials to prohibit the mailing of a writ because it was improperly drawn.[48] In a later case, prison officials in Tennessee limited the use of "jailhouse lawyers" in the prison, and the Supreme Court in *Johnson v. Avery* held that this could not be done unless a reasonable alternative for access to the courts was provided.[49]

The traditional rule in federal courts has been that indigent inmates are not automatically entitled to court-appointed counsel for federal *habeas corpus* proceedings, although the judge may appoint one if she or he desires. However, the American Bar Association recommends appointment in all *pro se* actions for post-conviction relief.

Appointment of counsel in a Civil Rights Act § 1983 action is left to the discretion of the court. Since these cases are civil, not criminal, in nature, there is no right to an appointed attorney.

In 1971, the U.S. Supreme Court decided its first case on law libraries, *Younger v. Gilmore,* where it upheld a court decision from California that had ordered law libraries for inmates. However, the court did not spell out in detail exactly what was required. *Know*

The Law Libraries Case [50]

The North Carolina Department of Corrections had been ordered in 1974 to submit either a plan to provide inmates with adequate law libraries or some reasonable alternative plan. The state submitted a three-part plan. First, the state would set up regional law libraries in prisons across the state. Second, the state would develop procedures for their use by inmates. And, third, the state would train inmate paralegals to staff each of the law libraries.

In affirming this decision in *Bounds v. Smith,* the Supreme Court specifically ruled that the "fundamental constitutional right of access to the courts requires prison authorities to assist inmates in the preparation and filing of meaningful legal papers by providing prisoners with adequate law libraries or adequate assistance from persons trained in the law." The North Carolina plan was ruled acceptable.[51]

The Supreme Court did not require that Departments of Corrections establish law libraries, if there was a reasonable alternative to provide inmates with assistance in the preparation and filing of meaningful legal papers.

However, in 1985, *Smith v. Bounds* was again examined by the U.S. District Court.[52] The court ruled that eleven years had passed since the court's initial order, and the state had still failed to implement the plan. Since the state was unable or unwilling to insure that its law libraries are constitutionally adequate to meet inmate needs, the court ordered an alternative method be established that must include, in some form, the assistance of counsel.[53]

It should be noted that Departments of Corrections need not allow jailhouse lawyers to function nor establish law libraries if adequate access is provided by some other plan (e.g., by attorneys).

The number of cases filed in the courts by prisoners has risen dramatically in the last twenty-five years. The Administrative Office of the U.S. Courts reported more than 22,000 prisoner petitions filed in federal courts on civil rights actions. This number does not include state tort suits. During a two-year period in a survey of state and federal systems with thirty-four systems responding, these thirty-four correctional systems identified 87 lawsuits that were lost to inmates and 161 settled resulting in monetary damages to inmate plaintiffs.[54]

One Inmate's Access to the Courts

Actual court documents filed in the Court of Common Pleas, General Division, Scioto County, Portsmith, Ohio:

Cleo V. Keaton, # 122–311
Plaintiff, Pro Se
              vs.   } Civil Action 81–460
T.C. Marshall, et al. Tower
Guards, et al., Defendants

This is the statement of facts in a civil suit in said ct.

1. At 12:30 a.m., I was standing in my cell, when I hear a clatter. I jumped out of my bed, to see what was the matter.
2. I seen a little fat guy, all dressed in red; The bullets were flying, I knew he would soon be dead. The searchlights were flashing. I saw by the light, Santa had a hacksaw, cutting on my window tonight.
3. From up on the roof, the reindeers came down; As Santa fell shot, was flopping on the ground. Santa jumped up; and I heard this sound. He and his reindeers are leaving this town.

Asking for:

4. A jury trial with all boys and girls who did not get their gifts that night after 12:30 a.m., December 25, 1981.
5. I ask $5,000 to be sent to the North Pole from each Defendant.
6. And $5,000 for the poor kids xmas fund.

Respectfully submitted,
Cleo V. Keaton # 122–311

Cleo V. Keaton, Plaintiff
              v.   } Case No. CIV 81–460
T.C. Marshall, Supt. et al.,   JUDGMENT ENTRY
Defendants

I examined the complaint to see what was the matter, But found it contained nothing but chatter. So, it occurred to my wondering mind what to do, Mr. Keaton, your complaint is dismissed, and the costs are assessed to you.

John B. Marshall, Judge

The courts are beginning to respond to the great numbers of suits that are frivolous or repetitive of unsuccessful claims already filed by the same or another inmate. Criminal contempt and new court-required reports are procedures sometimes being used to correct this abuse of the legal system.[55]

The right of meaningful access to courts applies to jail inmates as well as those in prison. Convicted inmates in jail, like sentenced prison inmates, have First and Sixth Amendment rights of access to the courts to challenge constitutional violations and illegal convictions.[56]

Pretrial detainees are entitled to counsel for their pending criminal charges, even if they cannot afford to pay for one. They have the right to represent themselves *(pro se)*. Since constitutional rights violations can occur in jail, pretrial inmates must be afforded meaningful access to the courts. Pretrial inmates, even though they usually have an attorney to represent them in their pending criminal case, may not be able to get that attorney to take on a case challenging the jail's conditions.

Problem 36

A. An armed-robbery victim identifies you as the person who committed the crime, and you are arrested by the police and released pending trial. You are told to work each day and be home at night. Make a list of the things you might do before trial to help your case.

B. Assume you are the same person in the preceding problem, but, instead of being released before trial, a bail of $5,000 is set and you can't pay it. Make a list of what you would do while awaiting trial in jail.

C. Look at the two lists you've compiled. Could a police officer on the street stop you from doing anything on the first list? Can jail authorities stop you from doing any of the things on your second list?

D. Inmate Brown was in a jail that had an adequate law library. He was allowed access to the library for forty-five minutes at a time, three times a week, but no research assistance was provided. Does this library program provide reasonable access to the courts?

E. Inmate Williams was confined in a maximum-security prison where prisoners were not allowed into the law library. Instead, they were taken to a library cell where guards brought law books requested by the inmates. The state also had funded programs of legal assistance. Does this procedure provide adequate access?

F. Are there any problems created by requiring the institution to
provide inmates with meaningful access to the courts?

FREEDOM FROM CRUEL AND UNUSUAL
PUNISHMENT

*"Excessive bail shall not be required, nor excessive fines imposed, nor cruel and unusual
punishment inflicted."*

Under the Eighth Amendment, an institution has the obligation to
furnish prisoners with adequate food, clothing, shelter, sanitation, medical care, and personal safety. These duties will be discussed on p. 140 in
the context of providing a basis for civil cases: either tort suits for
negligence or Section 1983 suits for constitutional violations.

Cruel and unusual punishments are those conditions of confinement
or punishments that involve the unnecessary and wanton infliction of
pain or are grossly disproportionate to the severity of the crime warranting imprisonment. The Supreme Court said that conditions of confinement must be judged under contemporary standards of decency.[57]

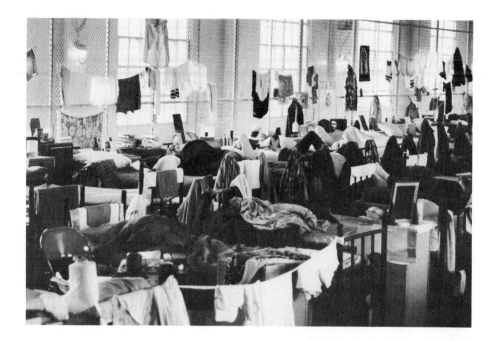

Certainly the most hotly litigated issue in corrections today is the question of conditions of confinement, which typically arises out of the overcrowding problem in many U.S. prisons and jails.

The Eighth Amendment ban on cruel and unusual punishment does not apply to pretrial detainees, because they cannot be punished at all.[58] However, the due process clause of the Fifth and Fourteenth Amendments which governs actions toward pretrial detainees, requires conditions that satisfy either the Eighth Amendment or even higher standards.

Problem 37 ◆ *The Case of the Crowded Prison*

The Facts

This maximum-security prison was built in the early 1970s. At the time of lawsuit, the institution was five years old and housed sentenced inmates, 67 percent of whom were serving life or first-degree felony sentences.

The Facility

This is considered a "top-flight, first-class facility." In addition to its 1,620 cells designed with one bed each, it has gymnasiums, workshops, schoolrooms, dayrooms, two chapels, a hospital ward, commissary, barbershop, library, an outdoor recreation field, a visitation area, and a garden.

Design Capacity

The institution was designed to house 1,620 inmates, one to a cell. Each cell measures sixty-three square feet and contains a bed, a night stand, a sink and toilet, a heating and air-circulation vent, a cabinet, a shelf, and a radio. There are windows in 960 cells.

After the prison was opened, the population increased to 2,300; 1,400 were double-bunked. Of these, 75 percent could spend much of their waking time outside their cells. The other double-bunked inmates spent even more time locked in their cells because of their classification.

The Case

Inmates file a Section 1983 class action lawsuit in the U.S. District Court claiming that double-celling inmates in cells originally built for one was cruel and unusual punishment and asking for an injunction to prevent the prison from double-celling.

The U.S. District Court found that, although the population had increased:

1. Food, air ventilation, and heating were adequate.
2. The noise level was not excessive.
3. There was no decrease in the availability of the library, school facilities, or visitation rights.
4. There was an increase in violence, but the increase was in proportion to the increase in population.
5. There was a proportionate decrease in the number of jobs available.
6. There was an increased delay in access to schooling.
7. Less psychiatric and social work help was available.
8. Double-bunked inmates had thirty to thirty-five feet each, which is below contemporary correctional standards.

Directions: Decide whether you agree or disagree with each of the following statements.

A   D   1. The facility is unconstitutionally overcrowded, because it provides less square footage than correctional experts and standards require.

A   D   2. The double-celling alone doesn't make the facility unconstitutional; but, taken together with the other problems, the prison conditions constitute cruel and unusual punishment.

A   D   3. Confining two persons in a cell or room this size constitutes a fundamental denial of decency, privacy, and personal security.

A   D   4.   Because the facility exceeds its design capacity, it is unconstitutionally overcrowded.

A   D   5.   Because the double-celling hasn't lead to deprivations of food, medical care, or other life necessities, conditions at the facility are constitutional.

A   D   6.   The amount of time inmates spend outside their cells during waking hours is an important consideration in this case.

In considering whether crowded institutions violate the Constitution, the courts will weigh many factors. Clearly, a key factor is the amount of out-of-cell time available to the inmates. The basic needs of food, clothing, medical care, adequate shelter, safety, and sanitation are also crucial. Many other factors influence the court's decision: age of the institution; amount of idleness versus educational, vocational, and work programs for inmates; visitation; and staffing levels. For example, in a state reformatory where cells were cramped, dirty, inadequately ventilated and poorly lit, double-celling amounted to cruel and unusual punishment.[59]

Specific Conditions

Personal Safety   When does the failure of correctional personnel to provide for the safety of inmates amount to cruel and unusual punishment? As discussed in chapter 2, intentional failure to protect (for instance, when an inmate under attack calls for help and the officers fail to respond) has resulted in a finding of cruel and unusual punishment in a number of cases.

An inmate claimed he had been sexually assaulted many times in the jail. The inmate claimed the sheriff was intentionally indifferent to the safety of inmates, because, for the past two years, he had allowed conditions to exist that resulted in inmates being constantly attacked by other inmates. The inmate sued the sheriff for damages for violating the inmate's right to be free of cruel and unusual punishment. The court said that if the inmate could prove his claim, he would have established a case of cruel and unusual punishment.[60]

An officer who, with callous indifference to an inmate's safety, assigns an inmate to a cell where it's likely the inmate will be assaulted can be held liable for cruel and unusual punishment.[61] Force used against an inmate in quelling a prison disturbance constitutes cruel and unusual punishment when it is applied maliciously or sadistically for the very purpose of causing harm.[62]

Inmates have claimed that their safety is protected under substantive due process of the Fourteenth Amendment. The Supreme Court has recently made it clear that the Eighth Amendment ban on cruel and unusual punishment is the primary source of substantive protection to convicted inmates where deliberate use of force is challenged as exces-

sive and unjustified. Due process affords convicted inmates no greater protection than the ban on cruel and unusual punishment. The Supreme Court did not express an opinion whether the rights of pretrial detainees might be greater than those who have been convicted of crimes.[63]

The U.S. Supreme Court resolved a conflict among the circuits in 1986 by ruling in two separate cases that negligent acts by correctional officers do not violate the due process clause of the Constitution.[64] Negligence is a civil tort that is actionable in state court, provided the state has consented to being sued. (See chapter 5 on Types of Civil Suits.)

In *Daniels v. Williams,* an inmate slipped on a pillow negligently left on a stairway by a deputy sheriff.[65] He sued the officer for a constitutional violation, claiming that this negligence deprived him of his liberty interest in freedom from bodily injury without due process of law.

In 1986 in *Daniels,* the Supreme Court ruled that the due process clause was intended to protect an individual from an abuse of power by government officials and that lack of due care (negligence) is no more than a failure to measure up to the conduct of a reasonable person. The Supreme Court denied the inmate the right to sue for a due process violation when only negligence is claimed; it felt that to rule that negligence violated the due process clause would trivialize the centuries-old principle of due process.

In *Davidson v. Cannon,* an inmate who was threatened by a fellow inmate sent a written note reporting the threat to the assistant superintendent, who read the note and sent it to a sergeant.[66] The sergeant, while informed of the contents, did not read it or notify other officers of the threat, and he forgot about it by the time he went off duty. Two days later, the inmate was attacked by the threatening inmate and received serious injuries. The injured inmate filed a Section 1983 suit claiming that his due process rights were violated by the negligent failure to protect him from the other inmate.

The state of New Jersey had passed a law providing that neither the state nor its employees are liable for any injury caused by a prisoner to any other prisoner. This statute prevented state tort suits for lack of care.

The Supreme Court rejected the inmate's claim when it ruled that due process protections are not triggered by lack of due care by prison officials. The due process clause does not require that there be a remedy when there has not been a deprivation of an interest protected by due process. However, the Court stated that injuries resulting from an unjustified attack by prison officers themselves or where officers stand by and permit an attack to proceed would violate due process.

Shelter Conditions of housing facilities for convicted inmates may constitute an Eighth Amendment violation or, for pretrial detainees, may be considered "punishment" in violation of the due process clause. Exactly how much space an inmate has a right to depends on many factors. The U.S. Supreme Court has said there is no absolute "one man, one cell" requirement under the constitution.[67]

Confinement for long periods without an opportunity for regular exercise has been held a violation as well.[68] Where overcrowding has forced prisoners to sleep in garages, barber shops, libraries, and stairwells and where they are placed in dormitories without shower and toilet facilities, courts have held that the Eighth Amendment was violated.[69] A general lockup of all inmates in a maximum security facility for five months amounted to an Eighth Amendment violation.[70] But the

Supreme Court ruled that double-bunking of pretrial inmates for less than sixty days in cells designed for one person in a new jail was not punishment in violation of due process.[71]

A number of federal courts have held that certain conditions of solitary confinement constitute cruel and unusual punishment. However, most courts rule that solitary confinement is not in itself an unconstitutional form of punishment where it is used: (1) to protect the general inmate population, personnel or individual prisoners; (2) to punish a prisoner for disobeying orders; or (3) to prevent escapes.[72]

Sanitation   An infestation of rats and vermin in the correctional institution may give rise to an Eighth Amendment claim.[73] Sanitation and health problems that included, among other things, an accumulation of sewage under the main kitchen and a serious rodent problem, constituted a violation in one prison system.[74]

However, in another case, a court found that unsanitary conditions that existed for about two and a half weeks in one prison were created by the inmates themselves during a prison riot. While the stench and filth would have constituted an Eighth Amendment violation if imposed by correctional personnel, the inmates' case was dismissed since the inmates had created the conditions.[75]

In 1985, a federal court of appeals found that vermin infested one prison and that the unsanitary conditions were inconsistent with the minimum standards of decency that prohibit unnecessary and wanton infliction of pain. In keeping with the Supreme Court's directions to defer to the expertise of correctional officials, the court agreed it need not tell the officials how to do the clean-up. The court can and should monitor what is being done in response to its order that the sanitary conditions violated the Constitution.[76]

Food   Inmates are entitled to a balanced diet. This has been measured in terms such as calories, nutrition, balance, and sufficient quantity.

Clothing   Inmates are also entitled to clothing that adequately covers them and is suitable to the climate. However, according to one case, inmates do not have the right to wear their own clothes instead of assigned jail garb.[77]

Medical Care   Inmates are entitled to adequate medical care at the same level of treatment a person on the outside would get. Negligence by doctors gives rise to possible medical malpractice actions in state courts.

Although courts generally agree an inmate is entitled to treatment prescribed by a qualified doctor, most courts have not interfered with the general quality of medical care unless it is truly inadequate. However, some courts have ordered institutions to improve medical services as well as other conditions.

A 1976 Supreme Court case, *Estelle v. Gamble,* established the standard that courts are to apply to determine if inadequate medical care constitutes cruel and unusual punishment. The court said that to state a claim of a constitutional violation, the inmate must show that the failure to provide adequate care was the result of "deliberate indifference to serious medical needs."[78] Pretrial detainees have at least the same rights under due process.

Deliberate indifference is established in any of three ways. One, an essential component of a health-care delivery system is missing. Two, there is no response to a serious medical need. Or, three, there is an extremely inadequate response to a serious medical need.

Serious medical needs are established when they are: (1) ordered by medical staff; or (2) obvious to laypersons.

A typical health-care delivery system includes an initial medical intake interview and screening upon admittance; a physical by a doctor within a few days; a system of frequent access (for example, sick call) available to inmates; visits by dental, psychiatric, psychological, and medical professionals, who are qualified to provide treatment, in sufficient numbers to meet inmate needs; direct treatment or immediate

---

**Correctional Law Project's
(American Correctional Association)
Model Correctional Rules and Regulations** *

II. ATTIRE

   A. Clothing

      1. Inmates shall be permitted to wear any personal clothing they wish unless it can be shown that such clothing may constitute a security problem.

      2. If an inmate is not allowed to wear personal clothing, he shall be provided with a sufficient supply of clothing suitable for the climate and adequate to keep him in good health.

      3. No clothing issued to an inmate shall be degrading or humiliating.

      4. All clothing shall be laundered on a regular basis.

---

* See Appendix D.

---

transportation services to provide for emergency medical problems; a classification system that takes into account inmate medical needs; procedures to handle mental, drug, and alcohol problems; accurate, confidential, and complete medical records; and training of staff in basic first-aid and emergency procedures.

Although no Supreme Court case has said prisoners with special problems, such as mental illness, alcoholism, or drug addiction, have a constitutional right to treatment, many cases have ruled that deliberate indifference to serious mental or emotional needs of inmates violates the ban on cruel and unusual punishment.[79]

A major Texas prison case established these seven minimum standards for mental health treatment in the state prison, providing a good checklist for mental health services.[80]

◆ There must be a systematic program for screening and evaluating inmates to identify those requiring mental health treatment.

◆ Treatment must entail more than segregation and close supervision of the inmate patients.

◆ Treatment requires the participation of trained mental health professionals, who must be employed in sufficient numbers to identify and treat, in an individualized manner, those treatable inmates suffering from serious mental disorders.

- ◆ Accurate, complete, and confidential records of the mental health treatment process must be maintained.

- ◆ Prescription and administration of behavior-altering medications in dangerous amounts, by dangerous methods, or without appropriate supervision and periodic evaluation are unacceptable.

- ◆ A basic program for the identification, treatment, and supervision of inmates with suicidal tendencies is a necessary component of any mental health treatment program.

- ◆ Any transfer of a prison inmate to a mental hospital requires certain due process procedures, including a hearing prior to transfer.[81]

A major medical concern today in prisons and large jails is the presence of Acquired Immunodeficiency Syndrome (AIDS). This disease, first identified in the United States in 1981, has been diagnosed in 28,246 persons in this country as of December 1, 1986.[82] Based on information gathered from all fifty states during the fall of 1985, approximately 420 cases of AIDS have been diagnosed in the nation's prisons.[83]

Legal questions are being raised regarding: the identification and diagnosis of persons with AIDS and AIDS Related Complex (ARC); the medical and institutional treatment of prisoners with AIDS and ARC and of those with a positive antibody test; the employment rights of staff with AIDS; and the employment rights of staff who must work with inmates and/or staff with AIDS.

Because the scope of the AIDS questions cannot be adequately addressed in this text, readers are advised to consult the publications and resources cited in the following text.[84]

Useful Information about AIDS

- ◆ Toll-free hotlines are made available by the Center for Disease Control in Atlanta: 1–800–342–AIDS for a recorded message and 1–800–447–AIDS for questions answered by a physician's assistant.

- ◆ Correctional guidelines for dealing with AIDS are available from the Center for Disease Control. Contact CDC in Atlanta at 404–329–3311.

- ◆ A free, two-page leaflet, "Facts about AIDS," is available from the Public Health Service, Office of Public Affairs, Room 721H, 200 Independence Ave. S.W., Washington DC 20201.

◆ Results of a national survey on how correctional systems are dealing with AIDS can be obtained from the American Correctional Association, 4321 Hartwick Road, College Park, MD 20740; 301–699–7600.

◆ "The AIDS Health Care Information Bulletin," published by the American Correctional Health Services Association, provides correctional staff with information on AIDS testing and management, legal information, educational materials, and general and clinical guidelines. ACHSA, Suite 917, 5530 Wisconsin Ave. N.W., Washington, DC 20815; 301–652–1172.

Many questions still exist about the use of inmates in medical experimentation. Of course, the participation must be voluntary, and Eighth Amendment problems are raised if there is any pressure on the inmate to participate. Many question whether "voluntary" experimentation is ever possible, because the inmate makes this decision while incarcerated, and cooperation may reflect favorably on his or her prison record.

Problem 38

In the following situations, consider whether Eighth Amendment rights were violated (in prison cases) or whether the due process clause was violated (in a jail situation). If not, consider whether a suit could be filed on other grounds.

A. A potentially dangerous x-ray machine was used on inmates after officials were warned of its danger.

B. The institution had a sick wing where it was extremely difficult for the patients to signal the staff and where there was inadequate patient observation.

C. A group of inmates gang raped another inmate while a correctional officer looked on from a hall but, because of fear, did not act to stop it.

D. A correctional officer saw Inmate Smith tampering with the lock on Inmate Bourgeois' cell and told Smith to move on. Later Smith threw a Molotov cocktail into the cell that burned over 30 percent of Bourgeois' body.

Problem 39

A. An inmate complains of chest pains and asks to see a doctor. You think he may be faking. What should you do?

B. An inmate was injured when a 600-pound bale of cotton fell on him while he was unloading a truck. He continued to work but, after four hours, became stiff and was granted a hospital pass. He was checked for a hernia by a medical assistant and sent to his cell. Within two hours, the pain was so intense he returned to the hospital, where he was seen by a nurse who prescribed pain pills, and he was then seen by a doctor.

The next day, a second doctor saw him, gave him pain pills and a muscle relaxant, and relieved him from work. A week later, the doctor continued the treatment program and, the following week, extended the treatment again.

At this point, despite the inmate's statement that his back hurt as much as it did the first day, he was certified for light work and given pain pills by the doctor. The inmate refused to work and was ordered to administrative segregation. A prison disciplinary committee sent him to a new doctor, who performed tests and prescribed a blood-pressure drug and pain relievers.

A month later, the inmate, still in administrative segregation, refused to work and requested to go on sick call. A medical assistant prescribed pain pills and high-blood-pressure medicine for thirty days. The inmate was again brought before the disciplinary committee, which ordered him to solitary confinement after the medical assistant testified the inmate was in "first-class medical condition."

Four days later, the inmate asked to see a doctor because of chest pains and blackouts. He was seen by a medical assistant, who ordered the inmate hospitalized. A new doctor ordered an electrocardiogram and began treatment for an irregular cardiac rhythm. The inmate was moved to administrative segregation. Three days later, he experienced pain and asked to see the doctor. The guards refused. The next day, they again refused his request. On the third day, he saw the doctor and filed a Section 1983 action claiming cruel and unusual punishment. Has the inmate been a victim of cruel and unusual punishment? Does he have grounds for any kind of lawsuit?

EQUAL PROTECTION OF THE LAWS

The Fourteenth Amendment: *"All persons born or naturalized in the United States and subject to the jurisdiction thereof, are citizens of the United States and of the*

State wherein they reside. No State shall make or enforce any law which shall abridge the privileges or immunities of citizens of the United States; nor shall any State deprive any person of life, liberty, or property, without due process of law; nor deny to any person within its jurisdiction the equal protection of the laws."

Equal protection requires that people who are in the same circumstances be treated alike under the law. Persons in similar circumstances who are convicted of the same crime, for instance, should be subject to the same sentencing laws. For example, a law that makes it possible for women to get longer sentences than men for the same offense would violate the equal protection clause of the Fourteenth Amendment.[85]

In one case, prison officials committed an inmate whom they believed to be insane to the state mental institution. This was done on the certification of one doctor (not a psychiatrist) without a hearing or judicial review of any kind. However, civilians were committed only after an examination by two qualified examiners, notice of the commitment proceedings, a hearing before a judge on the question of sanity with the right to call and confront witnesses, and a court order of commitment. The court could find no reasonable basis for classifying inmates and civilians differently with regard to commitment procedures and, therefore, held that the committed inmate's rights to equal protection had been violated.[86]

When classifications set out by the law involve what the court has called "suspect classes"—such as race, alienage, or nationality—or a "fundamental right"—such as the right to travel, to privacy, or to vote—the state must show a compelling state interest to justify different treatment. This means that it will be much more difficult for the state to treat people differently because of race, alienage, or nationality.

For example, racial segregation in institutions is unconstitutional because inmates, regardless of race, must be treated similarly. If the state were able to show a compelling state interest for segregation, such as a recent race riot, the court might find that a temporary period of racial segregation until the danger is past is constitutionally permissible.[87]

State and local governments must treat women offenders substantially the same way they treat male offenders unless there is an important reason for the different treatment. This requirement of substantial equivalence is sometimes called "parity." [88]

The courts have ruled that cost and administrative convenience are not important reasons to justify different treatment of male and female inmates.[89] Equal protection does not require identical treatment. Instead, it requires that the treatment of females be comparable to that of males.

State constitutions may also provide for equal protection of the laws. Sometimes, the protection provided by the state constitution is greater than that provided by the federal Constitution. For example, under California's equal protection right, the government cannot justify its different treatment of men and women inmates with an important reason. Instead, the government must have a compelling state interest in treating the groups differently, and this is a difficult justification to make.[90]

There have been other successful applications of the equal protection clause to jail and prison treatment of female and male inmates. For example, females successfully sued because they were not allowed to be trustees as the males were. Being a trustee granted greater freedoms and privileges.[91] A U.S. District Court Judge ruled that the females' claim could state an equal protection violation. The females had claimed that, unlike the males, they were housed in the prison without regard to age, custody degree, or the seriousness of offense.[92]

Males were denied equal protection under a state law that made only males responsible for expenses of hospitalization upon transfer from a community correctional center to a state mental hospital.[93]

Parity was provided under a schedule that allowed males use of the jail gymnasium seven hours a week and females three hours per week. Males outnumbered females ten to one.[94]

A male inmate's claim that he had the right to be sentenced to a female prison on the grounds that separate-sex facilities were unconstitutional was unsuccessful.[95] Also unsuccessful was a male inmate's challenge that female facilities were cleaner and neater than male facilities; it was determined that the difference rested with the inmates, not the jail authorities.[96]

Equal protection issues also arise where programs or services are established, and particular individuals are arbitrarily denied use of them. For example, if a visitation schedule is established at a correctional institution and Inmate Smith, for no specific reason, is not allowed visitors, her rights to equal protection have been violated. However, if she were denied visits because she is being properly punished for abuse of visitation or because of her security status, there would be no violation of equal protection.

Problem 40

  A. A female inmate was not provided with a work release program, although male inmates had such a program. Has this woman's right to equal protection been violated? If so, what remedies could the court order?

  B. One hundred twenty-four female inmates, of whom sixty-eight are sentenced, are housed in the women's jail, a concrete and steel structure first occupied in 1968. They sleep in dormitories designed to hold fifteen. They can have noncontact visits five days a week.

  Anywhere from two to ten of the sentenced inmates may be on work furlough at any one time; the average number is two or three. All other sentenced females perform such jobs as stocking food shelves and serving food, cleaning the kitchen, mopping and waxing floors, cleaning windows, collecting trash, sewing and mending clothes for male inmates, making mattress covers for jail beds, and serving as beauty operators. About fifty-seven work each day, although it only takes thirty-five to do all the work. The women can see a movie once a week and exercise outdoors on a thirty-three-foot-by-thirty-three-foot area on the jail roof four hours a day.

  There are ten times as many men in the county system, and they may serve their time in one of three county facilities. One thousand men are housed at the main male jail under conditions more harsh than those offered the females. About 45 percent of the men sentenced to jail serve their time in one of two branch jails. One branch, housing 233 males on an eight-acre campus, has unlocked barracks. All inmates have work furlough or assigned jobs in jail. Of the total, 59 percent are off campus while 41 percent on campus work, doing cooking, cleaning, yard maintenance, minor repairs, barbering, laundry, and clothes marking. There are no phones; the inmates can have one-hour contact visits each day of the weekend.

The other branch jail for the males has 100 inmates on a 100-acre farm. Almost all inmates work on the compound, raising crops and livestock. They can use the athletic field during the day and move about the one-and-a-half acre inner compound after dark. They can have one-hour contact visits on the weekend and get a monthly picnic. There are no phones.

The females sue the sheriff and the board of supervisors, claiming that they are denied equal protection of the law because of the privileges allowed the men. They ask the court to require that the sheriff and board: (1) permit females to be housed and detained at one of the branch jails now used exclusively for men; (2) apply the same criteria to female applicants as are applied to male applicants in determining eligibility for branch jails; (3) house eligible female inmates in a branch jail; and (4) permit females housed in branch jails to apply for, and be assigned to, available jobs on the same basis and under the same circumstances as males.

The sheriff argues that the arrangement is necessary to protect inmates from each other and to fulfill the statutory duty not to permit females to sleep, dress or undress, bathe, or perform eliminatory functions in the same room as males.

Does the county policy violate the equal protection clause? Does the jail policy treat people differently solely on the basis of sex? Does the government have an important governmental interest to justify its different treatment? If there is a violation, what remedy would you order?

SUMMARY EXERCISE ◆ LIMITING RIGHTS OF INMATES

Fill in the chart below, indicating whether you think correctional personnel may limit each of the listed constitutional rights either "greatly" (G), "some" (S), or "not at all" (NA).

Rights	How Much Can Each Be Limited?	Rights	How Much Can Each Be Limited?
Free Speech:		**Free Association:**	
Thinking	_____	Visitation	_____
Speaking	_____	Unions	_____
Writing	_____	Free Press	_____
Distributing & Writing	_____	Access to Courts	_____
Mail to Attorneys & Courts	_____	Freedom from Unreasonable Searches	_____
Mail to Others	_____	**Due Process:**	
Union Organizing	_____	In Disciplinary Hearings	_____
Union Membership	_____	In Transfer Hearings	_____
Religion:		In Classification	_____
Belief	_____	Freedom from Cruel & Unusual Punishment	_____
Reading	_____	Freedom from Discrimination	_____
Speaking	_____	**Freedom of Movement:**	
Religious Diets	_____	Inside the Institution	_____
Religious Dress	_____	Outside the Institution	_____
Starting New Religions	_____		

References

1. 441 U.S. 520, 99 S.Ct. 1861 (1979).
2. Id. at 1872, ftn. 16.
3. Rhodes v. Chapman, 452 U.S. 337, 101 S.Ct. 2392 (1981).
4. Bell v. Wolfish, Supra.
5. Block v. Rutherford, 468 U.S. 576, 104 S.Ct. 3227 (1984).
6. Id.
7. Medina v. O'Neill, 589 F.Supp. 1028 (S.D.Tex.1984).
8. Procunier v. Martinez, 416 U.S. 396, 94 S.Ct. 1800 (1974).
9. Id.
10. 418 U.S. 539, 94 S.Ct. 2963 (1974).
11. Dettmar v. Landon, 617 F.Supp. 592 (E.D.Va.1985), aff'd in part, rev'd in part 799 F.2d 929 (4th Cir.1986).
12. Gregory v. Auger, 768 F.2d 287 (8th Cir.1985), cert. denied ___ U.S. ___, 106 S.Ct. 601 (1985).
13. Guajardo v. Estelle, 580 F.2d 748 (5th Cir.1978), further proceedings, 568 F.Supp. 1354 (S.D.Tex.1983).
14. Glick v. Lockhart, 769 F.2d 471 (8th Cir.1985).

15. Hoppins v. Wallace, 751 F.2d 1161 (11th Cir.1985).

16. Wagner v. Thomas, 608 F.Supp. 1095 (N.D.Tex.1985).

17. Bell v. Wolfish, Supra. Also, Wagner v. Thomas, Supra; Kines v. Day, 754 F.2d 28 (1st Cir.1985).

18. Theriault v. Carlson, 495 F.2d 390 (5th Cir.1974), cert. denied 434 U.S. 871, 98 S.Ct. 216 (1977), rehearing denied 434 U.S. 943, 98 S.Ct. 441 (1977).

19. Theriault v. Silber, 453 F.Supp. 254 (W.D.Tex.1978).

20. Tyler v. Rapone, 603 F.Supp. 268 (E.D.Pa.1985).

21. Cole v. Fulcomer, 588 F.Supp. 772 (M.D.Pa.1984), rev'd 758 F.2d 124 (3d Cir.1985).

22. American Indian Religious Freedom Act, 42 U.S.C.A. § 1996.

23. Cochran v. Sielaff, 405 F.Supp. 1126 (S.D.Ill.1976); Walker v. Blackwell, 411 F.2d 23 (5th Cir.1969); Adams v. Carlson, 352 F.Supp. 882 (E.D.Ill. 1973), cause remanded 488 F.2d 619 (7th Cir.1973), on remand 368 F.Supp. 1050 (E.D.Ill.1973) and 375 F.Supp. 1228 (E.D.Ill.1974), aff'd in part, rev'd in part 521 F.2d 168 (7th Cir.1975).

24. 563 F.2d 741 (5th Cir.1977), further proceedings 599 F.2d 742 (5th Cir. 1979).

25. O'Bryan v. Saginaw County, Michigan, 437 F.Supp. 582 (E.D.Mich.1977), reversed on other grounds, 741 F.2d 283 (6th Cir.1984).

26. Fajeriak v. McGinnis, 493 F.2d 468 (9th Cir.1974).

27. Mabra v. Schmidt, 356 F.Supp. 620 (W.D.Wis.1973); Almond v. Kent, 459 F.2d 200 (4th Cir.1972).

28. Block v. Rutherford, Supra.

29. Brenneman v. Madigan, 343 F.Supp. 128 (N.D.Cal.1972).

30. Tate v. Kassulke, 409 F.Supp. 651 (W.D.Ky.1976).

31. 18 U.S.C.A. §§ 2510–2520.

32. Campiti v. Walonis, 611 F.2d 387 (1st Cir.1979).

33. Jones v. North Carolina Prisoners' Labor Union, Inc., 433 U.S. 119, 97 S.Ct. 2532 (1977).

34. Stroud v. Swope, 187 F.2d 850 (9th Cir.1951), cert. denied 342 U.S. 829, 72 S.Ct. 53 (1951); Berrigan v. Norton, 322 F.Supp. 46 (D.Conn.1971), aff'd 451 F.2d 790 (2d Cir.1971); Maas v. United States, 371 F.2d 348 (D.C.Cir. 1966).

35. Pell v. Procunier, 417 U.S. 817, 94 S.Ct. 2800 (1974) and Saxbe v. Washington Post Co., 417 U.S. 843, 94 S.Ct. 2811 (1974).

36. Houchins v. KQED, Inc., 438 U.S. 1, 98 S.Ct. 2588 (1978).

37. 468 U.S. 517, 104 S.Ct. 3194 (1984).

38. Bell v. Wolfish, Supra.

39. 746 F.2d 614 (9th Cir.1984), cert. denied 471 U.S. 1053, 105 S.Ct. 2114 (1985).

40. See California Penal Code, Section 4030.

41. McKinley v. Trattles, 732 F.2d 1320 (7th Cir.1984).

42. Bell v. Wolfish, Supra.

43. Storms v. Coughlin, 600 F.Supp. 1214 (S.D.N.Y.1984).

44. Security and Law Enforcement Employees, Dist. C. 82 v. Carey, 737 F.2d 187 (2d Cir.1984).

45. "Inmate Lawsuits," Contact Center, 1985.

46. Sullivan v. Ford, 609 F.2d 197 (5th Cir.1980).

47. Collins v. Schoonfield, 344 F.Supp. 257 (D.Md.1972), supp'd 363 F.Supp. 1152 (D.Md.1972).

48. Ex parte Hull, 312 U.S. 546, 61 S.Ct. 640 (1946).

49. 393 U.S. 483, 89 S.Ct. 747 (1969).

50. 430 U.S. 817, 97 S.Ct. 1491 (1977).

51. Id.

52. 610 F.Supp. 597 (E.D.N.C.1985).

53. In accord, Canterino v. Wilson, 562 F.Supp. 106 (W.D.Ky.1983); opposite ruling, Hooks v. Wainwright, 775 F.2d 1433 (11th Cir.1985).

54. "Inmate Lawsuits," Contact Center, 1985.

55. In re Green, 669 F.2d 779 (D.C.Cir.1981); Martinez v. Aaron, 570 F.2d 317 (10th Cir.1978).

56. Parnell v. Waldrep, 511 F.Supp. 764 (W.D.N.C.1981), supp'd 538 F.Supp. 1203 (W.D.N.C.1982).

57. Rhodes v. Chapman, Supra.

58. Bell v. Wolfish, Supra.

59. French v. Owens, 777 F.2d 1250 (7th Cir.1985).

60. Stevens v. County of Dutchess, N.Y., 445 F.Supp. 89 (S.D.N.Y.1977).

61. Smith v. Wade, 461 U.S. 30, 103 S.Ct. 1625 (1983).

62. Whitley v. Albers, 475 U.S. ___, 106 S.Ct. 1078 (1986).

63. Whitley v. Albers, Supra.

64. Daniels v. Williams, 474 U.S. ___, 106 S.Ct. 662 (1986) and Davidson v. Cannon, 474 U.S. ___, 106 S.Ct. 668 (1986).

65. Daniels v. Williams, Supra.

66. Davidson v. Cannon, Supra.

67. Bell v. Wolfish, Supra.

68. O'Bryan v. Saginaw County, Michigan, Supra.

69. Battle v. Anderson, 447 F.Supp. 516 (D.C.Okl.1977), aff'd 564 F.2d 388 (10th Cir.1977), rejected 497 F.Supp. 14 (D.P.R.1979), further proceedings 594 F.2d 786 (10th Cir.1979).

70. Jefferson v. Southworth, 447 F.Supp. 179 (D.R.I.1978), aff'd 616 F.2d 598 (1st Cir.1980).

71. Bell v. Wolfish, Supra.

72. Krist v. Smith, 309 F.Supp. 497 (S.D.Ga.1970), aff'd per curiam 439 F.2d 146 (5th Cir.1971). Hardwick v. Ault, 447 F.Supp. 116 (M.D.Ga.1978).

73. McIntosh v. Haynes, 545 S.W.2d 647 (Mo.1977).

74. Williams v. Edwards, 547 F.2d 1206 (5th Cir.1977), rev'd and remanded on other grounds 671 F.2d 892 (5th Cir.1982).

75. Carlo v. Gunter, 392 F.Supp. 871 (D.Mass.1975), vac'd and remanded on other grounds 520 F.2d 1293 (1st Cir.1975).

76. Hoptowit v. Spellman, 753 F.2d 779 (9th Cir.1985).

77. Wolfish v. Levi, 573 F.2d 118 (2d Cir.1978), rev'd on other grounds Bell v. Wolfish, Supra.

78. 429 U.S. 97, 97 S.Ct. 285 (1976).

79. Inmates of Allegheny County v. Pierce, 487 F.Supp. 638 (W.D.Pa.1980).

80. Ruiz v. Estelle, 503 F.Supp. 1265 (S.D.Tex.1980).

81. Ruiz v. Estelle, Supra; Vitek v. Jones, 445 U.S. 480, 100 S.Ct. 1254 (1980).

82. Based on telephone call to the Center for Disease Control's hotline, 1–800–477–AIDS, December 8, 1986.

83. National Prison Project Journal, No. 6 Winter 1985, p. 1.

84. Corrections Compendium, Vol. X, No. 8, p. 7, February 1986.

85. United States ex rel. Robinson v. York, 281 F.Supp. 8 (D.Conn.1978).

86. United States ex rel. Schuster v. Herold, 410 F.2d 1071 (2d Cir.1969), cert. denied 396 U.S. 847, 90 S.Ct. 81 (1969), further proceedings 440 F.2d 1334 (2d Cir.1971).

87. Washington v. Lee, 263 F.Supp. 327 (M.D.Ala.1960), aff'd sub. nom. Lee v. Washington, 390 U.S. 333, 88 S.Ct. 994 (1968).

88. Glover v. Johnson, 478 F.Supp. 1075 (E.D.Mich.1979).

89. Canterino v. Wilson, 546 F.Supp. 174 (W.D.Ky.1982), supp'd 562 F.Supp. 106 (W.D.Ky.1983).

90. California Constitution, Art. 1, Section 7; Molar v. Gates, 98 Cal.App.3d 1, 159 Cal.Rptr. 239 (4th Dist.1979).

91. Mitchell v. Untreiner, 421 F.Supp. 886 (N.D.Fla.1976).

92. Batton v. State Government of North Carolina, Executive Branch, 501 F.Supp. 1173 (E.D.N.C.1980).

93. McAuliffe v. Carlson, 377 F.Supp. 896 (D.Conn.1974), supp'd op. on other issues 386 F.Supp. 1245 (D.Conn.1975), rev'd 520 F.2d 1305 (2d Cir.1975), cert. denied 427 U.S. 911, 96 S.Ct. 3199 (1976).

94. Cooper v. Morin, 91 Misc.2d 302, 398 N.Y.S.2d 36 (1977), mod. in part on other grounds, aff'd in part 64 A.D.2d 130, 409 N.Y.S.2d 30 (4th Dept. 1978), mod. on other grounds, 49 N.Y.2d 69, 424 N.Y.S.2d 168, 399 N.E.2d 1188 (1979), cert. denied 446 U.S. 984, 100 S.Ct. 2965 (1980).

95. Dodson v. Indiana, 268 Ind. 667, 377 N.E.2d 1365 (1978).

96. Tate v. Kassulke, 409 F.Supp. 651 (W.D.Ky.1976).

CHAPTER 4

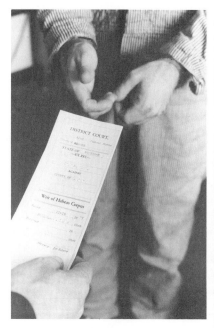

Due Process Rights of Employees and Inmates

The Fifth Amendment to the U.S. Constitution guarantees that *"No person shall be ... deprived of life, liberty or property, without due process of law."* This amendment requires the federal government to provide due process to persons facing the loss of rights or property. The same requirement of due process applies to states through the Fourteenth Amendment.

The concept of due process is intended to ensure that people do not lose their rights or property through unfair procedures. When people are threatened with being punished and losing their liberty in criminal cases, it is well established that they must be provided due process, which includes the right to written notice and the opportunities to present witnesses and other evidence, to confront and *cross-examine* their accusers, to be heard by an impartial judge, and to appeal a decision against them. However, in other situations where a person may lose property or some other liberty interest, it is not clear exactly how much due process must be provided.

In some cases, only partial due process applies. For example, when a student is being suspended from school, the courts have held that only a very informal hearing is needed and that no lawyer need take part. Reasons for not giving full due process rights in certain situations include high costs and the difficulty and complexity of following strict legal rules.

DUE PROCESS RIGHTS OF EMPLOYEES

Problem 41

Assume you are a correctional employee. One morning you arrive at work and are told to report to the superintendent's or warden's office. There you are told that the administration has evidence that you have been bringing drugs into the institution and have been distributing them to inmates. You are told that you are fired.

    A. What would you do in this situation?

    B. List all rights you believe have been violated.

In 1985, the U.S. Supreme Court decided that public employees classified as civil servants who could only be terminated for cause were entitled to hearings before they were fired.[1] The Court ruled that the state had created a property interest in continued employment. Due process protects that property interest. The procedures established by civil service did not adequately provide due process. Instead, prior to firing tenured employees who can only be terminated for cause, the employer must provide oral or written notice of the charges against them, explain the evidence that the employer has, and allow the employees to present their side of the story.[2]

In states with no civil service laws or other rules that require due process for employees, there are still three general situations where courts have required due process hearings: (1) when an employee is fired for exercising his or her constitutional rights, (2) when the firing takes away an employee's property rights, or (3) when the firing takes away the employee's "liberty."

The first occurs when an employee is fired for exercising a constitutional right. For example, assume that a correctional officer felt that conditions in an institution were dangerous, wrote a letter to the warden pointing this out, and was then fired for doing so. A court would probably hold that a hearing was required to determine if the employee was being fired because he or she had exercised the constitutional right under the First Amendment to petition for grievances. A claim that the action against the employee was motivated by or constituted discrimination would also require a hearing.

The second situation requiring hearings is when an employee's "property rights" are violated. Exactly what is meant by "property rights" is not clear. The best definition the U.S. Supreme Court has stated to date is that employees must show they have a "legitimate claim of right" to the job.[3] This situation arises when an employee has earned what is called "tenure." A probationary employee is unlikely to have this right; in one case, the courts held that, although a police officer was classified as "permanent," he still held his job "at the will and the pleasure of the city" and, therefore, had no right to a hearing before dismissal.[4] This issue, however, has not been clearly decided, since courts have ruled differently, and some have required hearings in similar situations. It should also be noted that higher-level unclassified employees, do not have greater rights in this regard. Such employees often are political appointees or work directly for an elected official; as long as they are "policy-making," confidential employees, they may be fired with even less due process than lower-ranking employees. However, the U.S. Supreme Court has ruled that employees, including a deputy sheriff in one case, cannot be fired solely because they are not members of one particular political party.[5]

A third situation requiring hearings is when the "liberty" of the employee is violated. Examples given by the Supreme Court include: (1) if the action seriously damages the employee's standing and associations in the community, or (2) if it imposes a stigma or other disability that forecloses the employee's freedom to take advantage of other employment opportunities.[6]

Mr. Faulkner, a correctional employee, was fired for holding a second job and using a department car for personal purposes. A supervisor interviewed by the press said, "Mr. Faulkner has not been completely honest, and a federal investigation is underway to determine if he has defrauded the government." The court held that Faulkner should be given a hearing because the statements made to the press hampered his ability to find another job and thus involved a "liberty" issue.

The procedures that must be provided to protect rights of an employee who is suspended, demoted, or laterally transferred have not been clearly decided by the courts. But, as has been noted, many localities have laws and rules that provide hearings and other due process protections.

Problem 42

A. Wilkins, a correctional officer, has just been appointed the union representative in his institution. Membership in a union is protected by the First Amendment right of association. He receives notice that the budget has been cut and his job has been terminated. Neither the state nor his institution has rules that require a hearing. Must he be given a hearing? Should he be reinstated in his job?

B. A prison had a rule that an employee could be fired for "cause." The prison doctor did not stay on duty for the entire sick call and was fired. Was this proper?

C. A correctional officer, during a period of unusual tension in an institution, left his post without permission and got into an argument with a deputy warden and threatened him. The officer was fired. Before this, he had a clean disciplinary record for twelve years. He filed suit in court protesting the firing. How should the court rule?

DUE PROCESS RIGHTS OF INMATES

Disciplinary Actions

Where an inmate faces the possibility of losing good time or being put in solitary confinement, the Supreme Court decided, in *Wolff v. McDonnell,* that due process requires inmates be given the following notice and opportunity to be heard:

1. written notice at least twenty-four hours before the hearing;

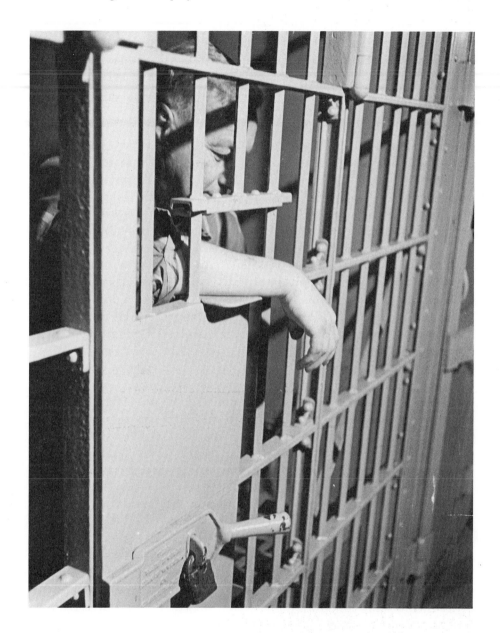

2. a written statement of the evidence and reasons for the proposed discipline; and

3. at the hearing, the right to call witnesses and present other evidence as long as this does not endanger institutional safety.[7]

One exception to the requirement of a hearing before confinement in segregation is in emergency situations. An attempted escape plus an assault on a guard justified temporary segregation without a hearing in one case.[8] Segregating forty inmates without an immediate hearing pending completion of an investigation into a series of serious assaults was permitted in another case, because the situation was an emergency involving a large number of inmates.[9]

The Supreme Court has said that, for disciplinary hearings, there is no constitutional right to counsel nor to cross-examine and confront the witnesses testifying against the inmate. However, if inmates are illiterate or the issues are complex, either a lawyer, another inmate, or a staff member must be appointed to provide adequate representation.[10]

In another U.S. Supreme Court decision, *Baxter v. Palmigiano,* the Court reaffirmed its earlier decision in *Wolff* that an inmate does not have a right to retained or appointed counsel at the hearing.[11] The Court also emphasized that the right to call, confront, and cross-examine witnesses lies in the sound discretion of the prison officials and that the officials need not give inmates written reasons for denying this right. The Court refused to discuss the issue of whether due process rights would be different if a prisoner faced a denial of privileges rather than loss of good time, though it seems to imply that due process might be less in that case.

More recent U.S. Supreme Court cases have elaborated on other important aspects of the disciplinary process. In *Ponte v. Real,* the Court ruled that due process requires that jail and prison officials at some point state their reasons for refusing to call witnesses requested by an inmate at a disciplinary hearing. They may do so either by making the explanation part of the administrative record or by later presenting testimony in court if challenged because of their refusal to call the requested witnesses.[12]

The Supreme Court set the standard for the amount of evidence required to find an inmate guilty of a disciplinary offense. In *Superintendent, Massachusetts Correctional Institute, Walpole v. Hill,* two inmates each received disciplinary reports charging them with assaulting another inmate.[13] At separate hearings, a board heard testimony from a prison officer and received his written report. According to the evidence, the officer heard some commotion in a prison walkway. Upon investigating, he discovered an inmate who evidently had just been assaulted and saw three other inmates fleeing down the walkway.

The board found the two inmates guilty and revoked their good time. These inmates filed a complaint claiming that the board's decisions violated due process since there was no evidence to support the board's findings. The Supreme Court ruled against the inmates. Although the evidence might be considered meager, the Court said, and there was no direct evidence identifying any one of the three fleeing inmates as the assailant, the record was not so lacking in evidence that the findings were without support or were otherwise arbitrary.

If sued for due process violations, disciplinary board members are entitled to qualified or limited, but not absolute, immunity from personal damage liability for their actions.[14]

The Fifth Amendment also states that people cannot be forced to be a witness against themselves. This has application at: (1) a criminal trial where the defendant has the choice to testify or to remain silent, and (2) other proceedings, criminal or civil, where a person may choose to remain silent as to matters that may be *incriminating.*

Inmates have the right to remain silent at disciplinary hearings in cases where the conduct they are charged with also constitutes a crime. However, prison officials are allowed to draw a negative inference from an inmate's silence at a hearing. They are not, however, permitted to find the inmate guilty solely on the basis of the inmate's silence. In other words, evidence other than the inmate's silence must be introduced to establish guilt.

Prison officials, like prosecutors, may have the option of granting *use immunity* to the accused. This means that the individual must testify but that nothing the individual says may be used in a subsequent criminal prosecution. Note that this does not mean the individual will not be tried for the criminal conduct; the immunity only limits the evidence that can be used to prove guilt.

An inmate was charged with possession of drugs. Assisted by a resident advisor, he pled guilty at a disciplinary hearing two days later. He was not informed before his plea that he had the right to remain silent, that he was entitled to counsel other than a resident advisor who was provided for him, or that anything he said at the disciplinary hearing could be used against him at a subsequent prosecution. He later sued, claiming he was forced to plead guilty because he was not given his Miranda warnings. The court held that an inmate need not be given Miranda warnings when disciplinary hearings are begun.[15]

However, this court and the Supreme Court in *Baxter* said that, if inmates are forced to give testimony against themselves, this testimony may not be used against them in subsequent criminal proceedings stemming from the same set of facts that gave rise to the disciplinary hearing.

An inmate was charged with two disciplinary offenses: possession of a hypodermic needle and syringe, and assault and use of abusive language on a correctional officer. He was also charged by state police with criminal violations regarding the incident. Nine days after pleading "not guilty" at his criminal court arraignment, he appeared before the institution's disciplinary board. He requested legal counsel and immunity regarding testimony he might give on the violations for which he was also facing state charges. Both requests were denied, and he refused to testify. The board found him guilty, and the inmate filed suit claiming constitutional violations for being denied counsel and being denied immunity. The court held that the inmate's rights had not been violated since he had not been automatically found guilty of an infraction by electing to remain silent. Thus, he was not being directly compelled to give testimony that might incriminate him in a later criminal proceeding.[16]

Several lower courts have dealt with the due process issue involved in the use of a drug-testing process called the EMIT procedure (Enzyme Multiple Immune Assay Technique).[17] In one case, the federal judge ruled that drug testing by use of the EMIT procedure indicating an inmate's recent marijuana use is enough, when confirmed by TLC (Thin Layer Chromatography test), to justify revocation of work-release status. To afford due process, all positive EMIT results should be confirmed by a second EMIT test or its equivalent.[18]

It should be noted that some state constitutions, corrections departments, and local institutions provide greater due process rights than the Supreme Court has required. In addition, courts in some states and federal circuits have provided greater due process rights than the U.S. Supreme Court; institutions within these states and circuits must follow their own rules unless those rules are legally changed.

Problem 43 ◆ Disciplinary Hearing Role-play

Disciplinary Report

Inmate: Roger Gray # 821–417

Date of Report: June 5, 1986
                   8:15 P.M.

Charge: Violation of Rule 65 from Rules and Regulations: As-
                   sault

                   Possible Penalty: 30 days in segregation; loss of good
                   time for period in segregation; or referral for prosecu-
                   tion

Facts:

On June 5, 1986 at approximately 5:15 p.m., I was sitting at my desk
in the visitors' area where I had just finished signing out the last visitor
for the day. I heard shouting coming from two inmates, Roger Gray
821–417 and Rodney Miller # 657–277, both of whom had been in
the visiting area for the last hour or so.

As I looked up, I saw Roger Gray with a knife, trying to stab Inmate
Miller. At that point, I yelled, "What's going on here?" The knife fell to
the floor, and I went over, picked the knife up, and placed Inmate Gray
in custody.

Gray had been a troublemaker for a long time, and this time he'd gone too far. The only other person besides Gray and Miller in the room at the time was another inmate who will back me up on this.

/s/ Officer William Jones

I have been given a copy of this report.

Roger Gray

Inmate

7:45 A.M., June 6, 1986

Hearing to be held: June 6, 1986
                    10:00 A.M.

Adjustment Board

Associate Superintendent Smith, chairperson
Major Carter
Psychologist Brown

Steps to follow during the hearing

1. Chairperson Smith should call the hearing to order. Hearing should begin by reading the charges aloud and the possible penalties. Then Smith should read the disciplinary report aloud.

2. The chairperson should ask Inmate Gray to relate his version of the story. First, Gray will request a postponement which the board should deny. Next, Gray will request legal counsel, and the board should deny this, stating that the law student who usually comes to the hearings is ill. Besides, since Gray is one of the jailhouse lawyers, he can articulate his story and defend his position adequately without counsel.

3. After Gray gives his version, the board may question him about his story.

4. Gray will ask to call and question Officer Jones, and the board should decide whether this will be allowed.

5. Gray will ask to call Inmate Miller, but the board will inform Gray that Miller is no longer housed in the jail, having been transferred early that morning to another detention facility.

6. Gray will then request the presence of ten witnesses from his cell block who will testify that Officer Jones has been hassling him for weeks. The board should deny this request.

7. Then Smith should ask Gray to step out of the room because the board wants to question a person in private who claims to have

seen the incident. The board does not tell Gray the name of this person. Gray will argue that he has the right to be present and question this person, and the board must decide whether to allow this.

8. The inmate (Reynolds) will then be called to testify.

9. The board will then consider whether Gray committed the assault. If the board finds Gray guilty, it must then decide his punishment. Board members should discuss this aloud. Chairperson Smith should state the decision to Gray.

Testimony of Roger Gray, inmate

Look, I've had hassles before with Jones. He's always trying to frame me. What really happened was that I was writing a letter to my lawyer about my case. I told her I was willing to turn state's evidence against Miller, who is the codefendant in my case. Anyway, Miller must have snuck up behind me and read the letter, because he suddenly snatched it out of my hands and pulled a knife on me.

I just tried to defend myself by fighting him off. I grabbed the knife from Miller and dropped it on the ground. That's when Jones came over and took me into custody, trying to say it was me who had the knife. I asked him to get the letter back from Miller, but he didn't do anything about it.

Steps for Gray to follow during the hearing

1. After the board reads the report aloud, you will be asked to give your version.

    First, you should request a postponement since you didn't see the report until 7:45, only two hours earlier, and you need more time to put together your case. The board will deny this request.

    Second, you should request someone to defend you, especially since, in this institution, law students usually represent people at hearings. The board will deny this.

2. You should then give your testimony.

3. After the board has asked you questions, you should ask to call and question Officer Jones. The board will decide whether or not to honor this request.

4. You should then request to call Inmate Miller, but the board will tell you that the inmate was transferred out of the jail earlier that morning.

5. You should then ask whether you may call ten other men from your cell block as witnesses. You should claim that all ten will be able to tell how Officer Jones is always hassling you and trying

to get you into trouble. You should demand to have all ten testify, not just one. The board will deny this request.

6. The board will then ask you to leave the room since it wants to call the witness (an inmate), referred to in the disciplinary report, who saw the whole incident. You should say you want to be present and question this man, that you think it's Reynolds, with whom you don't get along and who will say anything to hurt you.

   The board will decide to deny or grant your request to remain, hear Reynolds' testimony, and question him.

7. Inmate Reynolds will testify.

8. You will then be told the board's decision. If the board doesn't give reasons for the decision, you should request them.

Testimony of John Reynolds, inmate

It was right around 5:15 last night, and I had just finished talking to my lawyer in the visitors' room. I saw Gray and Miller arguing with each other. Gray is a born troublemaker. Why, just last week he was hassling me, accusing me of ripping off a carton of his cigarettes. He's just a bully, lots of trouble for most of the guys.

Anyway, I saw him with a knife trying to cut Miller. Miller tried to stop him and knocked the knife out of his hand. Then Jones came over and got Gray.

I know Officer Jones also thinks Gray is a troublemaker. I've heard him say he thinks Gray should spend more time in solitary.

And Miller's a good man. He and I have been buddies on the street since we were seven or eight years old. I know he wouldn't try to hurt anybody.

Transfers and Security Classifications

The Case of Montanye v. Haymes

After being sent from one maximum-security prison to another in New York, Inmate Haymes found himself several hundred miles from his home and family. Not only was he effectively separated from his only contact with the world outside the prison, but he was also removed from the friends he had made among the inmates at his earlier prison and forced to adjust to a new environment where he may have been regarded as a troublemaker. Contacts with counsel would necessarily be more difficult. A transferee suffers other consequences as well: The inmate is frequently put in administrative segregation upon arrival at a new facility; personal belongings are often lost; he may be deprived of facilities and medications for psychiatric and medical treatment; and educational and rehabilitative programs can be interrupted. Moreover, the fact of transfer, and perhaps the reasons alleged therefore, will be put on the record reviewed by the parole

board, and the prisoner may have difficulty rebutting, long after the fact, the adverse circumstances it suggests.

Haymes had been an inmate at Attica who worked as a law clerk. Because he allegedly violated prison rules by helping other inmates prepare their legal papers without first getting the warden's permission, he lost his position in the library. He circulated a letter addressed to a judge among the inmates, requesting signatures attesting that they were deprived of legal assistance due to Haymes' removal as law clerk. This letter, signed by eighty-two inmates, was seized, and Haymes was transferred to Clinton Correctional Center, another maximum-security institution.[19]

Does due process require that Haymes be given a hearing with notice, the right to present witnesses, to confront his accusers, before being transferred intrastate, and so on? The Supreme Court in 1976 said no, that there is no due process liberty interest of convicted inmates when transferred from one maximum-security institution to another in the same state, unless there is a right or justifiable expectation from state law that an inmate will not be transferred except for misbehavior or in certain specified events.

In explaining its decision, the Court said that as long as the conditions and degree of confinement are within the sentence imposed on the inmate, and otherwise do not violate the Constitution, the courts have no basis for reviewing prison officials' decisions.[20] It should be noted that at least one state has interpreted the due process clause of its state constitution as requiring due process rights for transfers.[21]

One situation that "otherwise violates the Constitution" is where the decision to transfer is an attempt to penalize the inmate for religious beliefs.[22] The Equal Protection clause has also been held to be violated when inmates are transferred to mental institutions without a hearing.[23] The U.S. Supreme Court has also held that, before inmates are transferred involuntarily to a mental hospital, they must be afforded full due process rights. The state created an expectation that inmates would not be transferred without a finding of mental illness for which no adequate treatment existed in the correctional facility. Also, the court found that transfers to mental hospitals stigmatize inmates and subject them to forced behavior-modification treatment, which involves a liberty interest protected by due process. To be involuntarily committed to a mental hospital, the inmate must fit the state criteria of danger to self or others or be gravely disabled.

The court required written notice; a hearing to inform the prisoner of the evidence relied on for the transfer; an opportunity to be heard and present evidence; a chance to present witnesses and to confront and cross-examine state witnesses, unless good cause exists to deny these rights; an independent decision maker; a written statement as to the evidence relied upon; qualified and independent assistance (not necessarily a lawyer); and effective and timely notice of all these rights.[24]

The Supreme Court's ruling on transfers applied to transfers to higher-security institutions as well.

Inmates suspected of arson were given security classification hearings with some due process rights. After they were transferred from a medium-security facility to a maximum-security facility, where conditions were less favorable, they sued, arguing that their due process rights had been violated by the fact that they were not given a hearing with the same rights provided at a disciplinary hearing. The Supreme Court said that due process rights were not available to inmates in classification transfers since the state had not granted prisoners a right to remain in the same prison to which they were originally assigned.[25]

What if the transfer is to another state? What if inmates are sent to institutions hundreds or even thousands of miles from their home? Are they entitled to due process before such a move? The Supreme Court reasoned that interstate transfers differ only in degree from intrastate transfers. Therefore, the U.S. Constitution provided no due process protection for an inmate in Hawaii transferred to a California prison.[26]

A state could create a liberty interest entitling inmates to due process protection by putting substantive limits on the officials' discretion. However, in this case, the state regulation allowed the administrator to transfer inmates out of state for any reason or for no reason at all. Therefore, the state created no right to due process.[27]

The Supreme Court has applied similar reasoning in deciding what due process was required before placing individuals in administrative

segregation in the same institution. Administrative segregation is a custody status separate from general population used to protect individuals or others and/or to promote and maintain order in the institution. Many times, conditions of administrative confinement are more restrictive than general population.

The general rule is that officials have great discretion in placing individuals in administrative segregation, provided there is a valid reason for doing so. The U.S. Constitution does not by itself give inmates a right to remain in the general population. A transfer to administrative segregation for nonpunitive reasons is well within the ordinary expectations of an inmate's confinement.[28]

Unless a state by its state law or institutional procedures creates a protected liberty interest, no due process is required prior to a transfer to administrative confinement.

The Supreme Court decided that this institutional policy created a liberty interest requiring some due process before transferring an inmate to administrative confinement: "An inmate may be temporarily confined to Close or Maximum Administrative Custody in an investigative status upon approval of the officer in charge of the institution where it has been determined that there is a threat of serious disturbance or a serious threat to the individual or others. The inmate *shall* be notified in writing as soon as possible that he is under investigation and that he *will* receive a hearing if any disciplinary action is being considered after the investigation is completed. An investigation *shall* begin immediately to determine whether or not a behavior violation has occurred. If no behavior violation has occurred, the inmate *must be released* as soon as the reason for the security concern has abated, but in all cases within ten days." [29]

When a state creates a due process requirement by its policy or statute, the following procedure must be provided: Inmates pending investigation of misconduct charges or those who present a threat to staff or others are entitled to an informal nonadversarial review of the evidence at the time of placement in administrative segregation.

This should include notice to the inmates of the charges; an opportunity for the inmates to present their views to the officials charged with deciding whether to transfer them to segregation (normally, a written statement from the inmate would be enough); and a review by the decisionmaker of the charges and then-available evidence.

The Supreme Court clearly stated that administrative segregation should not be used as a pretext for indefinite confinement of inmates; periodic review must take place—at least on a monthly basis.[30]

The rule on transfers for pretrial detainees may be different. In one case, a court of appeals ruled that the transfer of an inmate considered a security risk from a county jail to a state correctional institution did not require prior notice. However, the pretrial detainee was entitled to an opportunity to be heard by a state tribunal independent of the prison system after the transfer.[31] Some cases have also allowed pretrial or post-conviction transfers based on overcrowding, but pretrial detainees cannot be deprived of access to counsel.

Problem 44

   A. If a prison has no written policy regarding administrative segregation, can officials place inmates in this type of cell anytime they desire?

   B. If inmates are placed in administrative segregation for nonpunitive reasons—for example, their own protection—can they be kept in these types of cells during the rest of their confinement?

   C. Can an inmate be transferred to a prison hundreds of miles away, even in another state?

References

   1. Cleveland Board of Education v. Loudermill, 470 U.S. 532, 105 S.Ct. 1487 (1985).

2. Id.
3. Perry v. Sindermann, 408 U.S. 593, 92 S.Ct. 2694 (1972).
4. Board of Regents of State Colleges v. Roth, 408 U.S. 564, 92 S.Ct. 2701 (1972).
5. Branti v. Finkel, 445 U.S. 507, 100 S.Ct. 1287 (1980) and Elrod v. Burns, 427 U.S. 347, 96 S.Ct. 2673 (1976).
6. Bishop v. Wood, 426 U.S. 341, 96 S.Ct. 2074 (1976).
7. Wolff v. McDonnell, 418 U.S. 539, 94 S.Ct. 2963 (1974).
8. Mathis v. DiGiacinto, 430 F.Supp. 457 (E.D.Pa.1977).
9. Gilliard v. Oswald, 552 F.2d 456 (2d Cir.1977), petition for rehearing denied 557 F.2d 359 (2d Cir.1977).
10. Wolff v. McDonnell, 418 U.S. 539, 94 S.Ct. 2963 (1974).
11. 425 U.S. 308, 96 S.Ct. 1551 (1976).
12. 471 U.S. 491, 105 S.Ct. 2192 (1985).
13. 472 U.S. 445, 105 S.Ct. 2768 (1985).
14. Cleavinger v. Saxner, 434 U.S. ___, 106 S.Ct. 496 (1985).
15. Tinch v. Henderson, 430 F.Supp. 964 (M.D.Tenn.1977).
16. Roberts v. Taylor, 540 F.2d 540 (1st Cir.1976), cert. denied 429 U.S. 1076, 97 S.Ct. 819 (1977).
17. Wykoff v. Resig, 613 F.Supp. 1504 (N.D.Ind.1985); Kane v. Fair, 33 Cr.L. Rptr. 2492 (Mass.Superior Ct.1983); Jensen v. Lick, 589 F.Supp. 35 (D.N.D.1984); Storms v. Coughlin, 600 F.Supp. 1214 (S.D.N.Y.1984).
18. Wykoff v. Resig, Supra.
19. Montanye v. Haymes, 427 U.S. 236, 96 S.Ct. 2543 (1976).
20. Meachum v. Fano, 427 U.S. 215, 96 S.Ct. 2532 (1976).
21. Montanye v. Haymes, 427 U.S. 236, 96 S.Ct. 2543 (1976). Watson v. Whyte, 162 W.Va. 26, 245 S.E.2d 916 (1978).
22. Fajeriak v. McGinnis, 493 F.2d 468 (9th Cir.1974).
23. United States ex rel. Schuster v. Herold, 410 F.2d 1071 (2d Cir.1969), cert. denied 396 U.S. 847, 90 S.Ct. 81 (1969), further proceedings 440 F.2d 1334 (2d Cir.1971).
24. Vitek v. Jones, 445 U.S. 480, 100 S.Ct. 1254 (1980).
25. Meachum v. Fano, 427 U.S. 215, 96 S.Ct. 2532 (1976).
26. Olim v. Wakinekona, 461 U.S. 238, 103 S.Ct. 1741 (1983).
27. Id.
28. Hewitt v. Helms, 459 U.S. 460, 103 S.Ct. 864 (1983).
29. Id.
30. Id.
31. Yurky v. Eichenlaub, vacated and remanded 770 F.2d 1078 (3d Cir.1985), judgment vacated ___ U.S. ___, 106 S.Ct. 2240 (1986).

CHAPTER 5

The Role of Jail and Prison Personnel in a Typical Civil Lawsuit

As discussed in the preceding chapters, courts in recent years have become more willing to review occurrences in jails and prisons. It is important, therefore, for every employee to remember that what he or she does may ultimately be examined at some future time by a court or other agency.

While it is initially upsetting to be named as a defendant in a lawsuit, correctional employees who understand the civil process and the protections it affords may feel less threatened and apprehensive should they find themselves thus involved.

TYPES OF CIVIL CASES

There are two types of lawsuits occurring in a prison or jail setting in which a correctional officer may be involved:

1. Lawsuits challenging the conditions of confinement or the policies of correctional administrators (e.g., a claim that a jail is inadequately heated or that mail censorship violates an inmate's constitutional rights); or

2. Lawsuits challenging the conduct of the correctional staff (e.g., a claim that an officer's failure to protect an inmate resulted in a serious injury).

139

In the first case, the correctional officer *may* be a witness, but it is more likely that other corrections officials will serve as witnesses for the government. In the second case, however, the correctional officer is almost certain to be a witness (indeed, the most important witness) or one of the defendants. It is important, therefore, for correctional officers to understand the types of legal actions that can be brought by inmates challenging the officer's conduct. All these cases are civil cases.

The five major types of inmate lawsuits are summarized in the chart on p. 144.

State Tort Suits

A common form of action is a tort case, which is filed when the plaintiff (an inmate) claims that a wrong has been committed by the defendant (correctional employee). The plaintiff usually requests money damages for the wrong done. The inmate will have to show there was fault on the part of the defendant.

Which degree of fault is alleged and proven against the officer determines the type of lawsuit that can be filed, the type of money damages that can be collected, the availability of various defenses that officers may use, and the availability of attorney-fee awards against the correctional personnel.

Proof of negligence (simple negligence) requires showing that (1) a duty was owed to the person, (2) the duty was not fulfilled, and (3) the failure to fulfill the duty caused the injury and resulting damages. For example, a deputy is putting an inmate back in his cell. The deputy is distracted, and, as he closes the cell door, he catches the inmate's hand in the door, breaking three fingers. The deputy was negligent because he had a duty to provide for the safety of the inmate. He failed to fulfill this duty when he let his mind wander, and this failure caused the inmate's injury and resulted in *damages*.

Gross or wanton negligence is like simple negligence except that it requires some intent on the part of the actor to create a situation where it is likely that some injury will occur. If the officer in the preceding example played a little game when putting inmates in their cells—seeing how close he could come to the inmate's heels as he closed the door—and if he caught the inmate's hand in the door, his conduct would constitute gross negligence.

An intentional tort requires that the actor intended to cause the injury. Therefore, if the officer had a particular grudge against the inmate he was escorting back to the cell and deliberately slammed the cell door on the inmate's hand, breaking the fingers, the officer could be charged with an intentional tort.

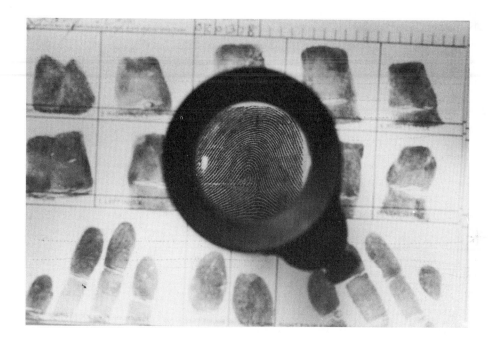

Some common intentional torts that may be committed in a jail or prison include assault, battery, false imprisonment, intentional infliction of emotional distress, and defamation.

Mental ✳ _Assault_ is an intentional act that puts another in reasonable fear of immediate touching that is unjustified. Examples include throwing a chair but not hitting a person and shaking a clenched fist in another's face.

Physical ✳ _Battery_ is the unjustified intentional act by a person to touch another in a harmful or offensive manner. For the tort of battery, all unjustified contacts that are offensive or insulting constitute battery. Consent of the person touched is a defense to battery. Examples of battery include spitting on a person, throwing a cup of urine on a person, and physically striking another. Many states have combined assault and battery as a single tort.

There are also the crimes of assault and battery. Criminal battery requires an act or omission with an intent to kill or injure or criminal negligence with resulting bodily injury or offensive touching of the victim.

Obviously, prison and jail officers have the right and duty to use force against inmates in certain circumstances. However, where the threat of force, the attempt of force, or the use of force is used unnecessarily, assault and/or battery have been committed.

✳ False imprisonment is the intentional confinement of a person without permission and without lawful privilege for an appreciable length of time, however short. Failure to release individuals when their terms have expired or when there is no legal basis for holding them constitutes false imprisonment.

✳ Words, gestures, or conduct that is extreme or outrageous and that results in demonstrable physical injuries establishes the tort of intentional infliction of emotional distress. Examples include an officer provoking a nervous breakdown by repeatedly telling a mentally unstable inmate that he was going to lock him up forever in the "hole" where he'd never see the light of day again or an officer conducting a pat search in an extremely abusive way with resulting bruises.

✳ *Sovereign immunity* is a special defense that federal and state governments, cities, and towns are immune from tort liability arising from governmental activities. Most jurisdictions have abandoned this doctrine in favor of permitting tort actions with certain limitations. This consent to be sued is generally set out in federal and state tort claims acts.

With the tremendous increase in the number of tort suits, the generous money judgments awarded against governments, and the apparent difficulty in obtaining or affording liability insurance, many states are passing tort immunity statutes, thus retracting consent to be sued for torts. For example, several states now provide that state and local governments and their employees are not liable for inmate injuries caused by other inmates.

Sovereign immunity does not apply to constitutional violations. Therefore, if the officer's action amounts to a constitutional violation, the inmate could sue the officer in a Section 1983 lawsuit, even if the lawsuit were barred in state court because of sovereign immunity.

State Constitutional Rights

State constitutional rights actions are more and more common. Generally, these claims are added to a Section 1983 lawsuit, alleging that the corrections agency or employee's conduct violates both the federal and state constitution. From 1970 to 1985, more than 250 state appellate opinions have provided greater protection of rights under state constitutions than the U.S. Supreme Court has under the federal Constitution.[1]

Civil Rights Act: Section 1983 Actions

This act has provided the basis for most claims by inmates that their constitutional rights have been violated, and these cases have usually been filed in federal district courts. However, the act applies in state courts, and some recent Section 1983 cases have been decided by state judges. Civil rights actions are referred to as Section 1983 lawsuits because the Civil Rights Act of 1871 is found in Title 42 of the United States Code under Section 1983. Section 1983 provides that:

> Every person who, under color of any statute, ordinance, regulation, custom or usage, of any State or Territory, subjects, or causes to be subjected, any citizen of the United States or other person within the jurisdiction thereof to the deprivation of any rights, privileges or immunities secured by the Constitution and laws, shall be liable to the party injured in an action at law, suit in equity, or other proper proceeding for redress.[2]

This act was originally passed to protect the civil rights of recently freed slaves in the South, but, since the 1960s it has been used by inmates and staff in suits against correctional officials. For the twelve-month period ending June 30, 1985, the administrative office of the U.S. courts reports more than 22,000 petitions involving civil rights filed by inmates in federal courts.

Parties to the Action   "Persons" who can be sued as defendants in a Section 1983 suit include state and local governmental employees. In the past, state and municipal governments had not been considered "persons" under the act; therefore, only individuals could be sued. However, a U.S. Supreme Court case now allows municipalities and local government units to be sued when they violate a person's constitutional rights through their "policy or custom."[3]

Liability and Defenses   In order to determine liability on the part of the official or local government agency, the officer has to be acting with authority of the state. Employees may be held liable in situations where they had authority to act for the state but went beyond the scope of that authority—for example, where correctional officers used too much force against an inmate. Employers, municipalities, and/or local governments may also be liable where the law or policy is in violation of the Constitution. In 1986, the U.S. Supreme Court held that a single decision of a county prosecutor authorizing police officers to proceed to enter a building was enough to constitute "county policy" and establish liability under Section 1983.[4]

Employers (the local government unit or sheriff, for example) will not be liable where the only connection between the employer and violation of the inmate's rights by the employee was that the employer hired the employee.[5] The employer must have taken some further action or failed to perform some duty in order to be liable. For example, an employer who failed to train employees properly in some facet of correctional work (for example, firearms training) could be held liable for rights violations by the employees resulting from this failure.

Chart of Types of Inmate Lawsuits

Types of Civil Cases	Grounds	Who May Be Liable	Where Case Filed	Special Defenses	Remedies
Tort Suits	Negligence Gross negligence Intentional torts	Employees committing tort; and/or supervisor if vicariously liable, head of institution, state or unit of government supervisor liable if action/inaction caused injury	State courts	Sovereign immunity (in some states)	Damages
Civil Rights Act (§ 1983) Suits	Violations of rights, privileges, or immunities given under Constitution or federal laws	Employees violating rights; supervisors or municipality where policy or custom causes injury	State or federal	Limited immunity	Damages, injunctions, declaratory relief
State Constitutional Rights Actions	Violation of state constitution	employees/ agency violating rights	State court; or federal court, if claimed with federal rights violations	Look to state law	Damages, injunctions, declaratory relief
Habeas Corpus Petitions	Illegal conditions of confinement	Custodian	State or federal court	None	Release from illegal conditions
Civil Rights of Institutionalized Persons Act Suits	Egregious or flagrant conditions in violation of rights, privileges, or immunities given under Constitution or laws, pursuant to a pattern or practice of deprivation	State, its political subdivision, official, employee, agent, or other acting for the state	Federal court	None	Injunctions (equitable relief)

Not every type of injury to an inmate can be remedied under Section 1983. Negligent acts by correctional officers do not violate the due process clause of the Constitution and, therefore, will not provide a proper basis for a Section 1983 lawsuit.[6] (See chapter 3 for a discussion of the rights of inmates under the Constitution.)

Many situations discussed in chapters 2 and 3—such as the use of too much force by correctional officers, failure to protect inmates from themselves or others, deliberate indifference to inmates' medical needs, or a violation of an inmate's established constitutional rights to free speech or religion—may form the basis for a Section 1983 suit. Remember, just because a suit is filed does not mean the claim is valid or that the correctional employee or agency lacks a defense that will be accepted by the court.

Although the "sovereign immunity" defense for actions in state court discussed on p. 142 does not apply in defense of a claim that constitutional rights were violated, the U.S. Supreme Court has recognized that in certain circumstances correctional personnel may have "limited immunity." The Court has held that if correctional officials take action "in good faith fulfillment of their responsibilities and within the bounds of reason," they may be shielded from liability (i.e., immune). However, the Court went on to say that this limited immunity will not protect officials where they "knew or reasonably should have known" or where their acts were taken with the "malicious intention to cause a deprivation of constitutional rights."[7]

The following is an example of a case where a federal court did find correctional administrators liable for violating a constitutional right.

An inmate was accused of violating the prison's disciplinary code. He was given a disciplinary hearing but was only allowed to admit or deny the charges. He was not given the opportunity to present evidence as required by Supreme Court decisions relating to due process. The inmate filed suit and was awarded $765 (or $25.50 per day for each of the thirty days he was in segregation) to be paid by the correctional administrators who were present at his hearing.[8]

Another U.S. Supreme Court case that gives some guidance as to when correctional employees may be held liable in Section 1983 suits is *Carey v. Piphus.*

An inmate sued prison officials on the grounds that they failed to mail various letters, including letters to legal assistance groups, news media, inmates of other prisons, and friends. This occurred in 1971 and 1972, when there was no established First Amendment right protecting the mail privileges of inmates.[9] (As was seen on p. 79, it was not until 1974 that the U.S. Supreme Court in *Procunier v. Martinez* firmly established some mail rights for inmates.[10])

In *Carey*, the Supreme Court ruled that corrections employees will not be held liable for violations of constitutional rights unless they knew, or should have known, that their conduct violated the prisoner's rights. The Court held that since the incident in question took place before it had been established that inmates have the right to mail letters to attorneys and others, corrections employees could not be held to know that their actions violated the inmate's rights.[11] Municipalities, however, are not entitled to this qualified immunity from damages liability in Section 1983 actions, even if the unconstitutional conduct was undertaken in good faith.[12]

Remedies   If successful in a Section 1983 lawsuit, the inmate can request and receive money damages and *injunctive* or *declaratory relief.* The Supreme Court will only sustain a nominal money damages award (such as a symbolic award of one dollar) unless the inmate can prove actual damages. The court will not presume that damage occurred to the inmate on the mere showing of a constitutional violation.[13]

Inmates can claim both compensatory damages (to compensate the inmates for their losses) and punitive damages (to punish the wrongdoers). *Injunctions* are court orders directing defendants to do or to refrain from doing a particular thing. For instance, the court could issue an injunction ordering the jail official to stop censoring inmate mail. Declaratory relief means that the court will announce the rights and liabilities of the parties without ordering anyone to do anything. For instance, jail officials decide to implement a new set of mail rules forbidding *Playboy* magazine, and the inmates believe them to be unconstitutional. The inmates might request a declaratory judgment that the court decide whether or not the pending rules meet constitutional standards.

Attorney's fees may be awarded to the prevailing party in Section 1983 lawsuits under 42 U.S.C.A. § 1988. This is important because there are often high attorney's costs even when only nominal damages are awarded to inmate plaintiffs.

The U.S. Supreme Court has held that the amount of attorneys' fees which can be awarded is not limited by the amount of damages recovered by plaintiffs.

In one case, the Court upheld an award seven times greater than the damages awarded.[14] In a previous case, the Court had listed the factors to be considered by courts in awarding attorneys' fees.[15] These included: (1) that a reasonable amount of time was spent by counsel, (2) the quality of the performance, (3) the success of the claims, (4) the complexity of the case, and (5) how much the fee award would advance the public interest. Based on these factors, attorneys have a right to request fees at "prevailing market rates."

These attorneys' fees cases have been criticized by some as making Section 1988 "a relief act for lawyers." Others praise them for helping ensure that lawyers will be available to civil rights plaintiffs who could not otherwise afford them.

Problem 45

A. If inmates have the choice of filing cases claiming violations of constitutional rights in either state or federal courts under Section 1983 of the Civil Rights Act, why do you think most are filed in federal courts?

B. For inmates, why might a federal civil rights action have advantages over a state tort claim?

Problem 46

Inmate Williams believed he was unjustly convicted and wished to file a habeas corpus suit in federal court. He did not have an attorney but had learned how to use a law library a few years before in another prison. Though the prison had a law library, he was in segregation for his own protection and, in May 1986, was refused access to the library until a new library was set up in the segregation unit in May 1987. Williams then used the new library and filed suit, winning his release in December 1987. His release was granted because of legal points he had researched in the law library and included in his court case.

A. Could Williams win a damage suit for violation of his constitutional rights? Why or why not?

B. What damages could Williams claim he had suffered?

Civil Rights of Institutionalized Persons Act

On May 23, 1980, Congress passed the Civil Rights of Institutionalized Persons Act. This law gives the federal government the authority to bring civil suits for equitable relief (injunctions), not damages, against a state, its subdivision, official, employee, or agent. To bring a suit, the Attorney General must have reasonable cause to believe that the defendant is subjecting persons confined in jails, prisons, pretrial detention facilities, or other correctional facilities to "egregious or flagrant conditions" in violation of federal law or the Constitution, causing them to suffer grievous harm. The deprivation must also be pursuant to a pattern or practice of resistance to the full enjoyment of those rights. Before a suit is brought in federal district court, however, the Attorney General must certify to the court that he has taken certain steps to notify and attempt a voluntary resolution of the conditions and that the need for the suit still exists. In practice, this act was rarely used by the Justice Department during the 1980s.

This law also gives the federal government the authority to join in any similar civil action by institutionalized persons already filed in any court. Again, the Attorney General must certify to the court that specific steps were taken to notify and remedy the conditions before joining in the suit.

Also of importance in this act is the section on administrative remedies. The federal government has set standards for the development and implementation of a grievance mechanism for adult correctional institutions. The standards at a minimum allow for:

- an advisory role for employees and inmates in developing and operating a grievance system;
- specific time limits for written replies to grievances;
- priority processing of emergency grievances;
- safeguards to avoid reprisals; and
- an independent review of the resolution.

The law allows for judges to suspend Section 1983 lawsuits for ninety days, requiring inmates to use the grievance procedure when such a procedure exists within the institution. (Public Law 96–247, 96th Congres, 1980). The grievance procedure must meet specific standards contained in the Department of Justice regulations.[16] The purpose is to give local officials a chance to remedy the problem first.

Habeas Corpus

Habeas corpus in Latin means "you have the body." Today, the term refers to a writ of habeas corpus, which directs a sheriff or a warden to produce an inmate under his or her control in a particular court at a particular place and time.

The procedure requires the inmate to file an application, petition, or *motion* for a writ of habeas corpus. The court may then issue an order to the sheriff or warden with custody of the inmate to show cause why the writ of habeas corpus should not be issued.

On the basis of the sheriff's or warden's response, the court may choose to dismiss the application, to issue the writ of habeas corpus, or to hold a hearing to obtain more facts and arguments before deciding on the merits of the application.

Habeas corpus can be used to attack the legality of the conditions of confinement. If a court agrees that the conditions are illegal, it will order the inmate released from those conditions. For example, an inmate in

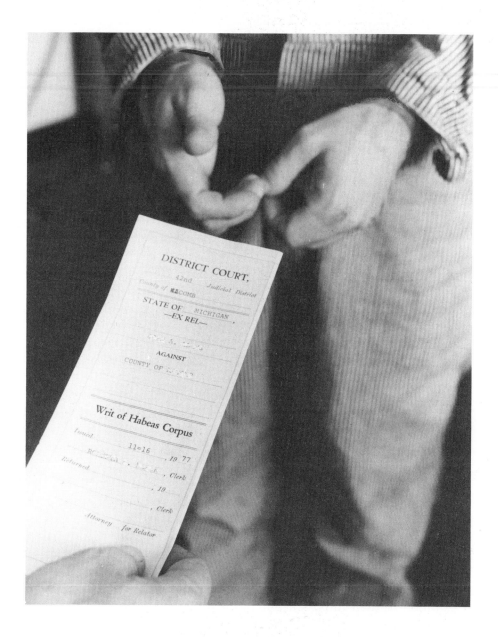

isolation who believes that the lack of access to legal materials, visitors, daily showers, and religious services in the chapel are illegal conditions may petition a court to issue a writ of habeas corpus ordering his release from isolation. If the court finds the conditions violate his constitutional rights, it can order his release or, at least, order the conditions be improved.

Habeas corpus is also used as a form of postconviction relief to challenge the legality of an inmate's conviction after the ordinary appeal process is completed. Money damages cannot be awarded in habeas corpus cases.

State Habeas Corpus   Many states have habeas corpus statutes. Under these, inmates file the application on their own behalf, and the action is brought against the person having legal custody of the inmates.

One problem for inmates is that this kind of action is civil, not criminal, so that many rights they would have had in criminal cases do not exist. For example, most states will not pay for legal counsel, and inmates usually do not have a right to be present at the hearing on the motion. Many states do not even require a hearing on the motion.

State prisoners are not entitled to raise the same issues again and again in their applications. Many states have specific restrictions on whether an issue can be raised again.

Federal Habeas Corpus   Federal habeas corpus is available to state prisoners under 28 U.S.C. § 2241(c)(3) only after they have exhausted all other state remedies. In addition, the motion must claim that the conditions of confinement violate an applicable federal law or a constitutional right.

As in the state system, there is a limit to the number of habeas corpus applications that can be filed for any particular issue.

PREPARATION OF REPORTS

Correctional officers are frequently witnesses or parties to an incident out of which a lawsuit will arise. Whenever an officer encounters an unusual incident, the officer should write up an incident report. Years later, it is possible that a lawsuit may be filed based on the incident. If the report was done well, this will help refresh the memories of those involved about the particulars of the incident and how it was handled. In addition to their importance in anticipating future lawsuits, reports help the institution perform its daily functions.

Lawsuits are started by the mere filing of a complaint. Since the truth of the claim is not investigated before filing and since there is generally a period of years within which to file a complaint (called the "statute of limitations"), correctional officers often encounter lawsuits involving incidents about which they have little or no recollection. Unless the officer documented the facts in a report at the time of the incident, there is little hope for a good defense. Additionally, if correctional personnel keep good reports and records and these are submitted to the

court as part of the official answer, the case may be dismissed at an early stage.

The American Correctional Association's Correctional Law Project says the following about preparation of reports.

> Clear, concise, factual reporting of incidents as they occur is important to the administration and the courts. The correctional officer is not only the first official involved in the resolution of important issues dealing with correctional institutions and offenders, but he may well determine the outcome. Reports filed at the time of an event are a valuable means of making an accurate record of an event while memory is fresh. This can be used later to refresh one's recollection and to permit superiors to review the officer's action without taking his time away from the job. Contemporaneous records can also be introduced in court proceedings under certain circumstances. The correctional officer's job is eased considerably by accurate "after-action" reports. None of these purposes can be served, obviously, by a record which does not exist.[17]

One Department of Corrections advises its employees to keep in mind these seven essentials and four requirements when preparing reports.[18]

Read to know

The Seven Essentials

- **What:** What happened? What occurred that made a written report necessary?
- **When:** When did it happen? Indicate by stating the exact time, day, and date.
- **Where:** Where did it happen? Give the location as accurately as the situation requires.
- **How:** How did it happen? This is the greater part of the report. It should describe what happened in chronological order.
- **Who:** Who was involved? All persons affecting and witnessing the incident must be indicated. What did each person say that was important to the incident?
- **Why:** Why did it happen? State only the facts. Don't guess or include something someone else told you unless you state who told you.
- **Action:** What action did you take? What was done with the evidence and with the inmate or inmates involved?

Read to know

The Four Requirements

- **Complete:** All essential facts are to be included so no additional information is required. *Right for nieve reader*
- **Clear:** Stick to the facts and use simple descriptive words. Keep your report in chronological order. Avoid using conclusions instead of facts. For example, "I used that amount of force necessary to maintain custody and control of the inmate" is a conclusion.
- **Correct:** Record only the actual facts. Make certain your words are spelled correctly and that you have used correct grammar. Keep your report neat.
- **Courteous:** Be cooperative and not hostile; be objective and fair.

A good report is a permanent record that reflects your training and personality. The report should be typewritten, if possible. If you can't type, then use a pen. If your handwriting is difficult for others to read, you should print your report carefully. Occasionally, additional copies of your report are requested by the administrators charged with making a decision, so be prepared to furnish the requested copies.

- **Profanity:** When profanity is to be quoted, each profane word should be spelled out. Since these utterances are recorded on a legal document, it is proper to give each word in full.
- **Authenticity:** When you are certain the report is correct and complete, your signature at its end indicates the report is authentic.
- **Check it over:** Before submitting a report, read it over twice; correct mistakes of grammar, spelling, and so on; and add any facts, names, or missing information. Hand it in only when you are sure it is clear and complete.

EVIDENCE

The following guidelines should prove helpful to correctional personnel in cases where some physical item connected with an incident is needed as evidence.[19]

Preservation of Evidence

Evidence should be picked up by the person who found it and not passed from person to person. If the evidence may later be used in a criminal trial, use a plastic glove or tongs to avoid adding your fingerprints to the item.

The evidence should be properly marked for identification (for instance, with the officer's initials and the date) and placed in some type of plastic container. The evidence should be turned over to the person responsible for storing things, normally with no more than two persons handling it before it is taken to court.

An item cannot be admitted into evidence unless you can show it was the same item found on the scene. One way this can be done is to prove exactly who had possession of the item at all times between when it was found and the day of trial. Therefore, each person who takes possession should mark his or her initials and the date on a tag attached to the evidence. (This is called "chain of custody.")

The evidence should be tagged with a memo stating when and where it was found and a physical description of the item so that the person who picked it up can identify it later on the witness stand.

Photographs

Photographs can be admitted in court as evidence under certain circumstances. At least two photos should be taken of the area where

the incident occurred and of each item. Vary the angle at which the photo is taken, while trying to get as much background in the photo as possible.

Put only the location, date, and time and the signature of the photographer on the back of the photo. Photos may be declared inadmissible if, for instance, you write on the back of the photo of an empty room "The room where Jones assaulted Officer Duke."

If the incident was an assault, you should take photos of the victim's wounds and also full-face and profile shots of the victim. If the incident involves a *homicide,* take both close-up and distance shots of the body. In most cases, close-up shots of very gory scenes will not be admitted into evidence because these photos may prejudice the jury.

If the incident constitutes a possible crime, you will want photos of the crime scene. If the crime occurred indoors, photograph all possible entrances and exits, including the outside of the building and walkways leading to and from the area.

If the scene is outdoors, be sure to get a building or permanent object in the background of the picture to establish relative distance, location, and what possible witnesses may have seen.

The Crime Scene

Certain special procedures should be followed if the incident may be prosecuted as a crime. If at all possible, seal off the area and identify as many witnesses as you can. (As soon as possible, write down the names of all witnesses and get signed, written statements from them.) If the area is a room or building, lock it up.

Post staff to guard the area. This staff member should keep a record of who enters and leaves the area and should seal off the area until the investigation is completed. No staff should be allowed to handle any evidence until each item has been photographed—unless, of course, the security of the institution is endangered.

Make a diagram of the area with measurements and make detailed notes of the findings. All staff who were near the crime scene should write a memo describing their movements and observations. These memos should be specific and state exactly what each staff member saw. (See section on writing reports.)

THE CIVIL PROCESS: HOW A LAWSUIT WORKS

The general steps taken in the civil process are as follows.

1. Complaint filed by plaintiff—Papers filed in court by the plaintiff or the plaintiff's attorney, claiming a civil wrong done by the defendant. The complaint sets out factual and legal *allegations* in support of the claim.
2. Answer by defendant—Papers filed by defendant (or defendant's attorney) that admit or deny the factual allegations made by the plaintiff and state the defense in the case.
3. Pretrial proceedings—Requests are filed for *discovery*—that is, an exchange of information between the parties.

4. Trial—Presentation of evidence by plaintiff and defendant.

5. Decision—Verdict by trier of fact, who may be jury or judge.

6. Judgment—Pronounced by the judge in favor of plaintiff or defendant.

7. Enforcement of judgment—Court forces the person against whom a judgment was decided to pay or take some action.

Complaint and Answer and Attorney Representation

Civil suits formally begin with the filing of a *summons* and complaint. In most states and in the federal system, a summons and complaint must be served at the same time; in other states, a summons is served in advance of the complaint. Basically, a summons is a document that brings the civil defendant—the person against whom damages or some other form of relief is sought—to the court. The person bringing the action is called the plaintiff. (In some states and with some kinds of legal cases, the plaintiff is called the petitioner, and the defendant is called the respondent.) A complaint spells out for the court and the defendant what civil wrong the plaintiff claims to have suffered. (See sample complaint on following page.)

The next step in the process is for the defendant, through counsel, to file an answer to the complaint. Because all courts have strict time limits within which complaints must be answered, correctional officers should notify their superiors and legal representatives immediately if served with a summons and/or complaint naming the correctional officers as defendants in a civil action arising out of an incident connected with their employment. The answer filed by the defendant's attorney will deny or admit each of the plaintiff's statements. (See sample answer on p. 160.) Failure to answer the complaint within the set time may result in a default judgment.

Where do correctional officers find attorneys to defend them when a complaint has been filed? In most cases, the state or local government will provide legal representation at no cost to the employee. (See chart on p. 162.) Generally, employees will be represented by counsel free of charge when sued for actions that fall within the scope of their employment and when they acted without fraud, corruption, or malice. Usually, the state Attorney General's office or the county or city attorney will conduct the defense. It is possible, although extremely rare, that a conflict of interest could arise among the various defendants in such a suit so that one office could not represent, for example, both the Department of Corrections and the employee. In the event of such a conflict, the officer

**State Court of the State of Maryland
Civil Division**

John Newman
Maximum Security Facility
Baltimore, Maryland 19234
                              Plaintiff
                    v.
Correctional Officer David
Austern
Henderson Youth Facility
Baltimore, Maryland 19767
                              Defendant   CA NO. 42–86
Correctional Officer James
Morgan
Maximum Security Facility
Baltimore, Maryland 19878
                              Defendant
Joann Gill, Director
Maximum Security Facility
Baltimore, Maryland 19878
                              Defendant

COMPLAINT

Plaintiff comes before this court and represents that:

1. The jurisdiction of this court is based on 82 Maryland Statutes 581.

2. Plaintiff is a resident of Maryland, presently residing in the Maximum Security Facility, Baltimore, Maryland. Defendant Austern is a Maryland resident presently employed by the Maryland Department of Corrections at the Henderson Youth Facility. Defendants James Morgan and Joann Gill are presently employed by the Maryland Department of Corrections at the Maximum Security Facility in Baltimore, Maryland.

3. On or about the night of August 29, 1986, Plaintiff Newman was housed in A Wing, Tier 1 of the Maximum Security Facility in Baltimore, Maryland. Correctional Officer James Morgan was on duty in A Wing, Tier 1 that same date. Officer Morgan maliciously and deliberately provoked Inmate Newman, taunting him about his wife's imminent death and the prison's denial of a furlough to be at her bedside. Officer Morgan then assaulted Inmate Newman by striking him with his fists. Inmate Newman attempted to defend himself.

4. Officer Morgan than gave a call over the radio for reinforcements. Officer Austern came to the scene and joined the assault on Inmate Newman. Correctional Officer Austern grabbed Inmate Newman and repeatedly banged Inmate Newman's head against the steel

bars of the cell nearest the assault while Correctional Officer Morgan held Inmate Newman by the legs. Inmate Newman was rendered unconscious by the blows, but the assault continued.

5.   As a result of this assault, Inmate Newman was severely and permanently injured.

6.   Defendant Joann Gill is the director of the Maximum Security Facility and at the time of the above-mentioned incident was directly responsible for the training of officers under her supervision. As director, she is responsible for the actions of her employees.

WHEREFORE, plaintiff requests that he be awarded

1.   Compensatory damages in the amount of $800,000, costs for pain and suffering in the amount of $3 million and $10 million for punitive damages.

2.   Any and all such further relief that the court deems proper.

Respectfully submitted,

J.D. Long
Attorney for Plaintiff
1727 S. Main Street
Baltimore, Maryland 19378
724–4521

should investigate the state's policy regarding the payment of attorney's fees for state or county employees.

Working with Counsel

Jail and prison staff should ask for the name of the attorney assigned to the case and should request that they be kept advised of the progress of the suit. Because attorneys work with many cases, clients often feel they are not getting the attention they deserve. If, even allowing for time constraints, personnel believe the attorney is not doing a good job preparing the case or is not being responsive to inquiries, they should discuss this with the supervisor and the agency. In the rare case where it appears likely that the officer may be found personally liable or be terminated if the case is lost, the officer may wish to consider hiring private counsel to assist in the defense.

On the other hand, personnel should follow the attorney's advice closely and be open and honest so that the attorney will have all the information needed to put on the best defense. The attorney-client privilege protects what is said between the client and attorney, so the attorney may not reveal this to anyone without consent.

Personnel can also assist the attorney by revealing the existence of pertinent records or the names of witnesses who could be helpful.

Discovery

Much of a civil case takes place before trial. Almost all these activities concern themselves with discovery—the process whereby the parties to the suit find out what the other side's case is all about. You should keep in mind that, in civil cases, unlike criminal cases, discovery is wide open. Within reason, a party can find out almost everything there is to learn about the other party's case. In all jurisdictions, the discovery rules are designed so that many cases will be settled out of court; the more the plaintiff and defendant learn about the strengths and weaknesses of each other's case, the more likely they will be to settle the case.

The three most common types of discovery devices employed in civil cases are: 1) *interrogatories,* 2) requests for production of documents, and 3) *depositions.*

Interrogatories are written questions that usually can be asked only of parties to civil actions (plaintiffs or defendants, not witnesses) and must be answered by the party under oath. In the hypothetical case of *Newman v. Austern, et al.,* the attorney for Newman might send the state's attorney representing the officers a set of these written questions, which the officers would be required to answer in writing under oath. The state's attorney will work with the officers and submit the answers to the opposing side. The state's attorney might likewise submit written questions that the inmate would be required to answer in writing under oath.

State Court of the State of Maryland
Civil Division

John Newman
                              Plaintiff

                    v.   CA NO. 42–86
Correctional Officer David
Austern, et al.
                              Defendant

ANSWER

Defendants Austern, Morgan and Gill come before this court and respectfully represent the following in regard to plaintiff's complaint in Civil Action 42–86.

1. Paragraph # 1 is admitted.
2. Paragraph # 2 is admitted.
3. The first two sentences in paragraph # 3 are admitted, but the following three sentences are denied.
4. The first sentence of paragraph # 4 is admitted by Defendants Morgan and Austern. Defendant Gill states she has no knowledge of that first sentence of paragraph # 4. The remaining sentences of paragraph # 4 are denied.
5. As to paragraph # 5, defendants deny that any injury sustained by the plaintiff was the fault of anyone but the plaintiff himself and state that they have no knowledge of the severity and/or permanence of the injury.
6. Defendants admit paragraph # 6, but deny that Defendant Gill is responsible for all actions of her employees.

COUNTERCLAIM

1. Paragraph 1 and 2 and the first two sentences of paragraph 3 of Plaintiff's complaint are incorporated herein. Inmate Newman was returning to his cell escorted by Correctional Officer Morgan (Defendant) after Newman had received an adverse decision on his furlough request. He turned on Officer Morgan and attacked him. Officer Morgan attempted to restrain the inmate but the inmate was too agitated to be restrained by Morgan alone. After calling the command center for assis-

tance, Officer Morgan continued his attempt to free himself from the inmate's hold. Officer Austern arrived shortly thereafter and the two officers succeeded in temporarily subduing the inmate. The inmate then broke out of the officer's hold, striking Officer Morgan and causing him injury. The inmate then lost his balance, fell and struck his head against the steel bars of the nearby cell.

WHEREFORE, Defendant Morgan, Austern and Gill respectfully request

1. That Plaintiff's claim for relief be denied in full;
2. That Defendant Austern be awarded $10,000 in damages for pain and suffering and compensatory damages for the injury he sustained;
3. That the court award any and such other relief as it deems fitting.

Respectfully submitted,

G.T. Swann
111 Second Avenue
Baltimore, Maryland 19727
281–7232

Requests for production of documents require the party served with the request to deliver to the other side all reports, examinations, memoranda, and so on concerning the case. Remember, all reports you prepare are probably obtainable by the other side (through discovery) if the matter described in the report is the subject of civil *litigation.* For example, the inmate's attorney would probably request the production of the institution's medical records on the inmate, any reports written, any photographs taken, and so on.

A deposition is an oral question-and-answer session involving either a party or a witness. It is conducted by the attorney calling the deposition. The questions and answers are recorded word for word by a court reporter, and the answers are given under oath. The person being deposed should concentrate on being as clear and accurate as possible in answering questions. If the answers at the deposition are different from any answers given at the later trial, the attorney can cross-examine the witnesses or party as to why the answers are different, and will try to make it look as though that individual is not telling the truth. Both witnesses and parties are entitled to have counsel assist them at any deposition.

If Officer Austern were deposed in the hypothetical case, he, his attorney, and the inmate's attorney would meet, probably at the office of the inmate's attorney. After being sworn in by the court reporter, Officer Austern would be questioned by the inmate's attorney about his actions, training, prior history in the corrections field, and his specific actions during the alleged assault.

Results of 1975 Survey: How Fifty States and Canada Provide Liability Coverage to Their Officers and Employees *

State	Legal Assistance	Indemni-fication	Comments
Alabama	Yes	No	
Alaska	Yes	Yes	No limit
Arizona	Yes	No	
Arkansas	Yes	No	
California	Yes	Yes	Punitive damages not covered
Colorado	Yes	Yes	Covers tort and § 1983
Connecticut	Yes	Yes	Immunity law
Delaware	Yes	No	Bills in drafting stage
Florida	Yes	Yes	
Georgia	Yes	No	
Hawaii	Yes	No	Provided by collective bargaining agreement
Idaho	Yes	Yes	
Illinois	Yes		
Indiana	Yes	No	
Iowa	Yes	Yes	Bill passed in 1975
Kansas	Yes	No	
Kentucky	Yes	No	
Louisiana	Yes	Yes	Indemnification limited to § 1983 actions
Maine	Yes	Yes	Ad hoc determination
Maryland	Yes	No	But may apply to Board of Public Works for help

Massachusetts	Yes	Yes	Limited to $10,000
Michigan	Yes	Yes	Not required to indemnify
Minnesota	Yes	No	Limited to tort actions
Mississippi	Yes	No	
Missouri	Yes	Yes	Limited to $100,000
Montana	Yes	Yes	
Nebraska	Yes	Yes	Ad hoc determination
Nevada	Yes	Yes	
New Hampshire	Yes	Yes	Broad protection given
New Jersey	Yes	Yes	No punitive damages
New Mexico	Yes	Yes	
New York	Yes	Yes	
North Carolina	Yes	Yes	Limited to $30,000
North Dakota	Yes	Yes	Bonding fund
Ohio	Yes	No	
Oklahoma	Yes	No	Limited to civil and civil rights actions
Oregon	Yes	Yes	
Pennsylvania	Yes	Yes	Legal help usually not provided in criminal cases; no limit
Rhode Island	Yes	Yes	Decided on case by case basis
South Carolina	Yes	Yes	Limited to $350,000
South Dakota	Yes	No	Provided up to $3,000 for legal assistance
Tennessee	Yes	No	
Texas	Yes	Yes	Bill enacted in 1975
Utah	Yes	Yes	
Vermont	Yes	Yes	Indemnification limited to $100,000 and discretionary
Virginia	Yes	Yes	
Washington	Yes	Yes	

West Virginia	Yes	No	
Wisconsin	Yes	Yes	Indemnification limited to $100,000
Wyoming	Yes	Yes	Limited to $250,000
Canada	Yes	Yes	

---

* Conducted by Correctional Law Project, American Correctional Association. Check in your state to see if there have been any changes since 1975.

The Trial

If a civil suit is not settled, there is a trial. In a criminal case, the burden is on the prosecution to prove the defendant guilty beyond a reasonable doubt; that is, almost all the evidence must point toward guilt. In a civil suit, the plaintiff also has the burden of proof, but the burden is less severe than in a criminal case. The plaintiff in a civil suit must prove his or her case by what is called the *"preponderance of the evidence,"*; that is, over 50 percent of the evidence must point toward liability. The reason for the greater burden in a criminal case is based on the historical legal requirement of greater certainty (provided by government evidence) when a person's freedom is at stake.

Instructions for Jail and Prison Personnel When Testifying at Trial [20]

Reprinted here is a set of instructions for correctional personnel when testifying at trial. Remember, these are general instructions and may not apply to all situations. Discuss these matters with your attorney before trial.

1. Dress appropriately. You are testifying in a court of law, so your clothes should suit the dignity of the occasion. Flashy or unusual clothing should not be worn. Men should avoid leisure suits. Women should wear everyday office apparel. Law enforcement officers should ask whether they should wear a uniform. When entering the courtroom, check with the attorney calling you or with the bailiff to see if any special order has been made concerning witnesses (for example, a special waiting room). Do not chew gum.

2. Do not engage in any discussion with jurors or prospective jurors. If you cannot avoid a casual, chance contact with a juror, take particular care not to discuss the case or anything connected

with it, and terminate the encounter as soon as you reasonably can. Furthermore, do not discuss the case with anyone while at the courthouse, especially when your conversation might be overheard by jurors, the opposing party or his attorney, or any other person. If you are in doubt whether you should discuss the case with someone who questions you, first consult with the attorney calling you. On the other hand, it is expected that you will have talked previously with a variety of persons—family members, friends, lawyers, and so on—about what you have seen or heard.

3. You will be questioned first by the attorney for the party calling you. Next, you will be cross-examined by the attorney for the opposing party, who might attempt to bait or embarrass you. The judge may permit further questioning by both sides and occasionally question you himself or herself.

4. Speak loudly enough to be heard by anyone in the courtroom. If there is a jury, aim your voice at the most distant juror. Sit up in the witness chair, and do not cover your mouth with your hand or engage in other nervous movements. These distract the jurors and the judge and detract from the effectiveness of your testimony. Don't shake your head in response to a question. Answer yes or no as appropriate.

5. Tell the truth simply and directly. Do your best to keep calm. A conscious effort to avoid the appearance of undue anxiety and tension will often help you. Be courteous at all times, regardless of how much you may be provoked by the questions asked of you. Remember, that by answering, you do not "adopt" the tone of the question. For example:

Question: Do you mean to sit there and tell me you discussed this case with the defendant's attorney before telling your story to the jury?

Answer: Yes, and the attorney told me to tell the truth.

6. Listen to the questions asked of you. Wait for the questioner to end before answering. Make sure that you understand what is asked. If you don't understand the question, say so. Pause briefly before answering, and think about the question. This is especially important if a considerable length of time has passed since the events about which you are to testify occurred. In such a case, if you answer too quickly, it may suggest that your answers have been memorized or perhaps are even made up. By pausing, you will also give your attorney the chance to object to improper questioning by the other side.

7. Answer only the question asked. Keep your answers short. Do not give a long, narrative statement unless specifically called for. Don't volunteer information. Try to answer yes or no to questions on cross-examination, but don't be afraid to ask the judge if you may explain any answer, particularly if the answer you have given may be misleading because of the way the question was asked.

8. Testify from memory. Don't attempt to memorize earlier statements. You may consult notes you made at the time or shortly after the event. These will normally become available to opposing counsel. If you made a mistake in an earlier statement, change it. It is not *perjury* for you to change an earlier statement that was not intentionally inaccurate or mistaken (whether it was made under oath or not).

Question: Then you admit that you are changing your sworn statement?

Answer: Yes, because . . . (explanation of why).

9. You do not have to know the answer to every question asked of you. If you do not know the answer, simply say that you do not know. If you cannot recall, simply state that you do not remember. Above all, don't guess or engage in speculation.

10. Expect to be asked about earlier statements you may have made, whether recorded by a court reporter (such as a deposition), handwritten, or even oral. If, during cross-examination, an attorney reads to you from earlier testimony or an earlier statement, listen carefully to what is read before answering the questions.

11. During cross-examination, do not look at your attorney or the attorney for the side calling you. Maintain eye contact with the attorney questioning you and with the judge or the jurors.

12. If you are asked questions about what the plaintiff or someone else may have said, do not be afraid to state the actual language he or she used, even if it includes profanity or obscenities.

13. Above all, be sincere and candid. Even if you have to admit mistakes, it is quite probable that your testimony will be accepted if you are responsive, courteous, and sincere. It is only human to make mistakes, and the judge or jury will appreciate and understand your honesty in admitting them. In no event, should you display hostility toward the opposing attorney, nor should you attempt to "get smart." You will only undermine your testimony if you do.

14. Upon conclusion of your testimony, you will be excused. It is preferable that you leave the courtroom and not remain in the spectators' section, because you may give the impression you have an improper interest in the outcome of the case. If there are special reasons why you wish to stay in the courtroom, consult with the attorney who called you.

Payment of Damages and Costs

After the trial, the factfinder (either jury or judge) decides the verdict, and the judge announces the judgment for either the defendant or plaintiff. At this time, the defendant, for example, might be found liable for an injury to the plaintiff, and the judge announces a judgment for the plaintiff in the amount of a certain sum of money.

In the hypothetical case of *Newman v. Austern, et al.,* the judge could order Officer Austern to pay $50,000 to the injured inmate. Where will Officer Austern get this money? Will the state pay or *indemnify* the officer? (Note the chart on pages pp. 162–164 that lists the indemnification policies of the various states as of 1975.)

As you will see, most states will pay for any judgment entered against an officer for acts that occur within the scope of employment and that do not involve fraud, malice, or corruption. No money actually comes out of the officer's own pocket. In other words, the courts are unlikely to punish officers personally if they use good judgment and just make an honest mistake. Additionally, attorneys will invariably sue and try to collect money judgments from those with the most money. That means that they will sue the agency or, at least, high-ranking officials as well as the officers. It is very rare that a court judgment is executed against line officers or mid-level supervisors; therefore, they rarely have to pay out of their own money. However, most jurisdictions will not pay punitive damages against officers. Punitive damages, as the name implies, are intended as punishment. They are damages awarded not because an officer was negligent, forgetful, or even incompetent but, rather, because the officer acted in a wanton, reckless, malicious, or fraudulent manner.[21] Recently, at least one state has changed its state law to allow the payment of punitive damages ordered against an employee where certain criteria demonstrate that it would be in the state's interest to do so.[22]

It may also be possible to obtain liability insurance through the agency or union. However, such policies should be examined closely to be sure that they provide the proper coverage. Often liability policies sold to law enforcement agencies cover mainly street-type situations, such as false arrest. They usually do not cover punitive damages. State law often will prohibit insurance from paying punitive damages. Officers need to be sure to have an attorney (who is knowledgeable about state law and corrections) review any policy that personnel may be considering for themselves or staff.

Inmates may also request, in addition to other forms of *relief*, that the state pay their attorney's fees. This decision is left to the discretion of the court. In the absence of a statute, courts normally do not grant the winning party attorney's fees unless the losing party is guilty of *bad faith*. If the plaintiff is successful, the attorney usually takes a percentage of the money the plaintiff wins. However, in Section 1983 lawsuits, if the plaintiff prevails in the case, the defendant generally must pay for the plaintiff's attorney's fees at the attorney's normal, reasonable rate.[23] This is important because, in lawsuits where the damages may not be great (for instance with nominal damages of $1.00), the attorney's fees may amount to $10,000 or more.

Hutto v. Finney, discussed before, demonstrates how a court may award attorney's fees.

After a series of cases involving hearings, appeals, and several remedial orders to correct the unconstitutional conditions of the Arkansas penal system, the District Court in Arkansas ordered the defendants—the commissioner of corrections and the Arkansas Board of Corrections—to pay $20,000 in counsel fees to the inmates' attorney out of Department of Corrections funds. The court based its order on a finding of bad faith because several improvements it had ordered in prison conditions had not been made. The Court of Appeals ordered an additional $2,500 in attorney's fees for the appeal to be paid by the defendants under the Civil Rights Attorney's Fees Award Act of 1976, and it did not make a finding of bad faith as to the appeal.

The Supreme Court upheld both awards, finding that they were within the discretion of the court and that the award for bad faith served the same purpose as a fine for civil contempt, which might incline the Department of Corrections to act so that further litigation would be unnecessary.[24]

It is also possible for the court to order an inmate who loses a case to pay the state's attorney fees. Obviously, this is unlikely to occur except in a few cases where inmates with money file suit.

The Supreme Court in two decisions in 1985 distinguished between suits filed in an individual's "personal" capacity and those filed in an

individual's "official" capacity.[25] In *Brandon v. Holt,* the Supreme Court ruled that a judgment against public servants "in their official capacity" imposes liability on the entity (for example, the city) that they represent.[26]

In *Kentucky v. Graham,* six persons were falsely arrested following the warrantless raid of the home of James Graham, whose son was a suspect in the slaying of a state trooper. The suspect was not one of the six. The six persons were beaten, terrorized, and illegally searched.[27] Three of these individuals then sued the officers individually for excessive force and the commonwealth for fees, should the lawsuit be successful. The case was settled in favor of the arrestees for $60,000. They then moved that the commonwealth pay their attorney's fees and costs.

The Supreme Court ruled that the government entity (here, the commonwealth) could not be required to pay the attorney's fees and costs, since the defendants were sued in their individual or personal capacities. To establish personal liability in a Section 1983 action, it is enough to show that the official, acting under color of state law, deprived another of a federal right. More is required in an official capacity action. For the government to be liable under Section 1983, the entity itself must be a "moving force" behind the violation. In this case, there had been a "complete breakdown" of trooper discipline, rather than the carrying out of a governmental policy.[28]

Treatment of Inmate Plaintiffs or Witnesses

Correctional officers and officials should be careful not to show any hostile feelings or take any retaliatory actions against inmates involved in the cases. To deny them privileges or threaten them verbally or physically would constitute interfering with the court process and might result in the officers or officials being charged with contempt of court or a separate criminal offense. In addition, if a judge involved in a case is told that such actions are taking place, this may contribute to a decision against the institution and its employees.

Problem 47

Inmate Jones and Officer Smith have a confrontation in the institution over a discipline charge. A fight takes place. Jones is hurt and files suit against Smith. Two weeks later, Smith sees Jones, and Jones yells, "I'll see you in court!" What should Smith do in this situation?

Problem 48 ◆ Representation and Indemnification Case Study

Bruce Easly, a jailhouse lawyer in a state prison, was being escorted from a disciplinary hearing by Officer Jim Beam. Easly had just been found not guilty of using verbal abuse against Officer Fields, Jim Beam's best friend.

Officer Beam states that, as he was escorting the inmate back to his cell, the inmate got agitated and attempted to assault him. He further states that he ordered Easly to his cell, that Easly told him to "shove it," and refused to move in the direction of his cell. Beam then applied a "come-along" hold to Easly and escorted him to his cell.

Easly claims that Officer Beam told Easly that he may have gotten off this time, but he was going to make real sure to get him on something soon and that Easly had "better watch his back." Easly also denies that he told Beam to "shove it."

Twelve hours later, Easly saw medical personnel who determined that he had multiple fractures of the right arm due to the come-along hold applied by Beam. Beam received a written reprimand from his supervisor, Foster Grant, for failing to write a "Use of Force" report and for failing to obtain necessary medical services.

A. Easly files a tort suit in state court claiming assault and battery, negligence in not obtaining medical care for twelve hours, and supervisory liability for failure to train and negligent assignment.

   1. Whom will Easly name as a defendant for each claim?

   2. Will the state's attorney represent the defendant(s)? Why or why not?

   3. Will Easly win against the defendant(s)? Why or why not?

   4. If Easly wins, what will he win?

   5. If money is awarded against the defendant(s), who will pay?

   6. Who will pay Easly's attorney's fees?

B. Easly files a federal civil rights lawsuit, claiming his right to due process and freedom from cruel and unusual punishment were violated.

   1. Whom will he name as a defendant in the suit?

   2. Will the state's attorney represent the defendant(s)? Why or why not?

   3. Will Easly win against the defendant(s)? Why or why not?

   4. If Easly wins, what will he win?

     5. If money is awarded against the defendant(s), who will pay?

     6. Who will pay Easly's attorney's fees?

  C. Beam is being investigated by a grand jury.

     1. Will the state's attorney represent Beam during the grand jury proceeding? If there are further criminal proceedings? Why or why not?

References

1. State v. Jewett, 34 Cr.L. 2409 (1985).
2. 42 U.S.C.A. § 1983.
3. Monell v. Department of Social Services of the City of New York, 436 U.S. 658, 98 S.Ct. 2018 (1978).
4. Pembaur v. City of Cincinnati, 475 U.S. ___, 106 S.Ct. 1292 (1986).
5. Monell v. Department of Social Services of the City of New York, Supra.
6. Daniels v. Williams, 474 U.S. ___, 106 S.Ct. 662 (1986) and Davidson v. Cannon, 474 U.S. ___, 106 S.Ct. 668 (1986).
7. Procunier v. Navarette, 434 U.S. 555, 98 S.Ct. 855 (1978).
8. Mack v. Johnson, 430 F.Supp. 1139 (E.D.Pa.1977), aff'd 582 F.2d 1275 (3d Cir.1978).
9. 435 U.S. 247, 98 S.Ct. 1042 (1978).
10. 416 U.S. 396, 94 S.Ct. 1800 (1974).
11. Carey v. Piphus, Supra.
12. Owen v. City of Independence, Missouri, 445 U.S. 622, 100 S.Ct. 1398 (1980).
13. Carey v. Piphus, Supra. Also see Memphis Community School District v. Stachura, 477 U.S. ___, 106 S.Ct. 2537 (1986).
14. City of Riverside v. Rivera, 477 U.S. ___, 106 S.Ct. 2686 (1986).
15. Hensley v. Eckerhart, 461 U.S. 424, 103 S.Ct. 1933 (1983).
16. 28 C.F.R. Part 40.
17. ABA and ACA Correctional Law Project, "Legal Responsibility and Authority of Correctional Officers," 1976.
18. Adapted from materials from the District of Columbia Department of Corrections.
19. Adapted from an article written by Dempsy Johnson and published by the *American Journal of Corrections,* Nov.-Dec. 1977, with permission from the publisher.
20. Taken from "General Instructions to First-Time Witnesses." Prepared by W. Eric Collins, Deputy Attorney General, San Francisco, California 92102. Copyright pending. Written reproduction without the express, prior written permission of the author is forbidden.
21. Smith v. Wade, 461 U.S. 30, 103 S.Ct. 1625 (1983).
22. California Government Code Section 825 (1985).
23. 42 U.S.C.A. § 1988.
24. 437 U.S. 678, 98 S.Ct. 2565 (1978).

25. Brandon v. Holt, 467 U.S. 1204, 104 S.Ct. 2384 (1985); Kentucky v. Graham, 473 U.S. 159, 105 S.Ct. 3099 (1985).
26. Brandon v. Holt, Supra.
27. Kentucky v. Graham, Supra.
28. Kentucky v. Graham, Supra.

Glossary of Legal Terms

Abridge infringe upon; take away from; restrict.

Adversary Proceeding a hearing at which opposing sides present their point of view.

Affirm to agree with the decision of a lower court.

Agency a government administrative division that is responsible for enforcing laws and promulgating rules for regulating a particular subject area, i.e., corrections.

Allegation statement of fact from one side's point of view that will be proven true or false at a hearing or trial.

Allege to claim an unproven fact to be true.

Amendment a change or addition to a bill or law.

Appeal a procedure of review by which a higher court or agency examines lower court decisions for errors and either upholds the lower court's decision or reverses it.

Appellate a type of court that hears cases appealed from lower courts.

Arbitrator a person with the power to hear and settle a dispute.

Arraignment appearance of a criminal defendant before a judge in court, where the charges are read and a plea is entered. In a misdemeanor case, this may be the first appearance. In a felony, it is usually after a grand jury indictment is issued.

Assault a physical attack or threat of attack by a person with the apparent ability to carry out the threat.

Attest swear that something is true; usually in writing.

Bad Faith acting in a manner that indicates a person is intentionally misleading, deceiving, or is prompted by some bad motive.

Bail the security provided as assurance that a person under arrest will return to court.

Balancing Test a decision-making process used by the court to balance two opposing interests and resolve the issue.

Bar to prohibit or keep from. **175**

Beneficiary a person who receives money or property through a trust, will, insurance policy, or contract.

Binding enforceable or having the force of law.

Bond a form of money bail required by the courts to allow the accused person to be released from jail before trial.

Breach a violation of a law or obligation.

Brief a written argument stating one's case that is filed with an appellate court.

Burglary breaking and entering a building with the intent to commit a felony.

Capital Crime a crime for which one can receive the death penalty.

Censor to keep part or all of something from being written, published, or looked at.

Charge to formally accuse of a crime.

Circuits the thirteen divisions of the United States that each contain U.S. District Courts and a Court of Appeals that hears appeals from the District Courts in the circuit.

Civil Case a lawsuit brought against a person or organization asking for money damages or for court orders requiring that action be taken or stopped.

Claim lawsuit.

Collective Bargaining a process for labor and management to meet and work out an agreement to settle labor conditions and disputes.

Confiscate to seize by or as if by authority.

Conjugal Visit a visit in a correctional institution that allows an inmate and spouse to have sexual intercourse.

Constitutional Claim a claim in a lawsuit alleging violation of a constitutional right.

Contraband certain goods, the possession, import, or export of which is illegal.

Contract a legally enforceable agreement between two or more persons; each party promises to do some act or make some payment.

Corporal Punishment physical punishment such as whipping or beating.

Counsel an attorney.

Criminal Case a court proceeding to determine the guilt or innocence of one charged with an act that violates a penal law.

Cross-Examination the opposing side's right to question a witness during a trial or hearing.

Custody to have responsibility for the care and keeping of a person or thing.

Damages money asked for and awarded by a court in a civil case to a person for injuries or losses suffered through the fault of another.

Declaratory Relief a court judgment that states the rights of the parties regarding some legal matter; no action is ordered, nor are damages awarded.

Defendant a person who is alleged to have committed some wrong; a party in either a civil or criminal suit.

Deposition a form of discovery where a witness' sworn statement or testimony is taken out of court, usually with the lawyers for both sides present and a court reporter recording everything said; the manuscript of the proceeding is also a deposition.

Discovery the pretrial process of obtaining information from the other side in a lawsuit; depositions and interrogatories are two types of discovery.

Due Process of Law a phrase in the Fifth and the Fourteenth Amendments meaning that persons have a right to be treated fairly before the government takes away their liberty or property.

Enact to put into effect as a law.

Enjoin to order a person or organization by court decree to stop doing something; injunctive relief.

Equal Protection phrase in the Fourteenth Amendment meaning that persons in similar situations have a right to be treated equally under the law; not discriminated against.

Felon person who has been convicted of a felony.

Felony a crime punishable by a prison sentence of a year or more.

Findings a court's rulings or decisions on questions of law or fact, i.e., the court "found" that . . .

Fraud a deliberate deception for unfair or unlawful gain.

Grand Jury a group of twelve to twenty-three people who hear preliminary evidence and decide whether a person should be formally charged with a crime.

Grounds basis or foundation for an action; legal basis for filing a lawsuit.

Habeas Corpus Latin phrase meaning "You have the body." A legal procedure (writ) available to anyone to challenge an illegal custody or confinement.

Homicide act of killing a person.

Immunity protection from prosecution or liability.

Incarcerate to confine in a jail or prison.

Incriminate to make a person look guilty or to show involvement in a criminal offense.

Indemnification a security given by one person or institution to reimburse another for loss or damage.

Indictment a formal charge by a grand jury, accusing defendant of a crime.

Information a formal accusation of a crime made by a public official such as a prosecuting attorney (like indictment, but not made by grand jury).

Infraction a violation of a rule.

Injunction a court's order directing a person not to do something or to perform some act.

Injunctive Relief relief from some particular act granted by a court order; to *enjoin*.

Injuries wrongs or damages to a person's body, property, rights, or reputation.

Instrument a tool, weapon, or document.

Instrumentalities tools or other items involved in carrying out some act.

Interrogatories a set of written questions directed to the opposing side in a lawsuit.

Invalid not enforceable or legally binding.

Jail an institution that holds accused persons prior to trial (pretrial detainees) and sometimes short-term convicted inmates.

Judgment a court's final decision in a case.

Jurisdiction the geographical or subject area in which a court, judge, or official has authority to act.

Jurisprudence the study of law and the philosophy of law.

Larceny stealing.

Lawsuit proceeding in which one person or organization sues another for money damages and/or asks for a court order; a civil action or civil case.

Legislature an official group of people who make and pass laws.

Liability a legally enforceable obligation or responsibility for something, as for a debt or harm to another.

Litigation a lawsuit.

Lobby to influence a legislator's vote on a bill or to persuade a legislator to write a bill.

Malice the intentional doing of a wrongful act without just cause or excuse and with an intent to inflict an injury.

Malpractice a lack of competence or care (negligence) on the part of professionals (e.g., doctors and lawyers) that causes injuries to their patients or clients.

Mandamus a proceeding brought to compel a person to do some act; a court order that some action be taken.

Mediator a person who helps two or more parties settle a dispute (like an arbitrator in arbitration hearings).

Misdemeanor a crime punishable by less than a year in prison.

Misdemeanent a person guilty or convicted of an offense which is less serious than a felony (usually carrying a sentence of less than one year).

Mock simulated; an imitation or make-believe act, such as a mock hearing.

Motion a request to a judge or decision maker to make a ruling or take some action on a matter involved in a lawsuit.

Negligence the failure to take reasonable care in doing something or in not doing something for someone to whom a duty is owed, thereby causing harm or injury to that person.

Nolo Contendere Latin phrase meaning "I will not contest it"; a type of plea to a criminal charge, in which the defendant does not directly admit guilt but also does not contest or deny the charge, and therefore accepts whatever punishment is ordered.

Parole supervised release from prison before the full sentence is served.

Penitentiary a prison.

Perjury lying under oath.

Petit Larceny theft of an item worth less than a certain sum; the amount varies from state to state.

Petition a formal document containing a request in the redress of some wrong.

Plaintiff a person who files a lawsuit against another.

Precedent an appellate court's decision on a question of law that guides future decisions of lower courts on similar questions of law.

Presentment a hearing where persons arrested for misdemeanors appear before a judge to be read their rights and to make their pleas.

Pretrial Detainees persons charged with a crime who are being held in jail until trial.

Prison an institution for the incarceration of felons.

Probation a form of sentence by which a person convicted of a crime is allowed to remain in the community instead of serving a jail or prison sentence.

Pro se to appear in court and represent oneself without a lawyer.

Prosecute to proceed against an individual, in a criminal case; i.e., the state prosecutes.

Proximate Cause the legal cause of an accident or injury.

Quell to subdue, quiet.

Recidivist a repeat offender; a person who has been convicted of a crime more than once.

Relief court-ordered compensation or assistance given to the party that wins a civil lawsuit; this includes money damages or court orders and may be referred to as declaratory relief or injunctive relief.

Remand to send back, as when a court sends (remands) a case back to a lower court for some further determination.

Remedy a correction of some wrong; a compensation for an injury or harm.

Reverse to set aside (void) a lower court's decision and make a new one.

Rule a court's decision on a matter.

Scope of Authority subject areas of responsibility and control.

Sovereign Immunity a government's freedom from being held liable for money damages in civil actions.

Statute law made by legislatures.

Summons a court paper notifying a person that he or she is being sued and requiring his/her presence in court at a certain time and place.

Third Party Custody a form of bail in which a person is put under the care or supervision of another person not involved in the criminal charges.

Tort a civil wrong involving a breach of some obligation that results in monetary loss or injury to a person.

Undue too much; excessive; improper.

Use Immunity protection given by the government to a person in return for testifying; it prevents the government from using any statements made during that testimony, or any evidence discovered because of the testimony, as evidence in a later criminal prosecution of that witness.

Verdict   a decision by a judge or jury in a case.

Void   not enforceable or valid; not legally binding.

Warrant   a paper issued by a judge or magistrate authorizing some action, such as an arrest or a search of some premises.

Writ   a court order requiring that a certain act be done or that a certain act not be done.

Specific Amendments to the Constitution

Amendment 1

Congress shall make no law respecting an establishment of religion, or prohibiting the free exercise thereof; or abridging the freedom of speech, or of the press; or the right of the people peaceably to assemble, and to petition the Government for a redress of grievances.

Amendment 4

The right of the people to be secure in their persons, houses, papers, and effects, against unreasonable searches and seizures, shall not be violated, and no Warrants shall issue, but upon probable cause, supported by Oath or affirmation, and particularly describing the place to be searched, and the persons or things to be seized.

Amendment 5

No person shall be held to answer for a capital, or otherwise infamous crime, unless on a presentment or indictment of a Grand Jury, except in cases arising in the land or naval forces, or in the Militia, when in actual service in time of War or public danger; nor shall any person be subject for the same offense to be twice put in jeopardy of life or limb; nor shall be compelled in any criminal case to be a witness against himself, nor be deprived of life, liberty, or property, without due process of law; nor shall private property be taken for public use, without just compensation.

Amendment 6

In all criminal prosecutions, the accused shall enjoy the right to a speedy and public trial, by an impartial jury of the State and district wherein the crime shall have been committed, which district shall have been previously ascertained by law, and to be informed of the nature and cause of the accusation; to be confronted with the witnesses against him; to have compulsory process for obtaining witnesses in his favor, and have the Assistance of Counsel for his defense.

Amendment 8

Excessive bail shall not be required, nor excessive fines imposed, nor cruel and unusual punishments inflicted.

Amendment 9

The enumeration in the Constitution, of certain rights, shall not be construed to deny or disparage others retained by the people.

Amendment 10

The powers not delegated to the United States by the Constitution, nor prohibited by it to the States, are reserved to the States respectively, or to the people.

Amendment 11

The Judicial power of the United States shall not be construed to extend to any suit in law or equity, commenced or prosecuted against one of the United States by Citizens of another State, or by Citizens or Subjects of any Foreign State.

Amendment 13

Section 1. Neither slavery nor involuntary servitude, except as a punishment for crime whereof the party shall have been duly convicted, shall exist within the United States, or any place subject to their jurisdiction.

Amendment 14

Section 1. All persons born or naturalized in the United States are subject to the jurisdiction thereof, are citizens of the United States and of the State wherein they reside. No state shall make or enforce any law which shall abridge the privileges or immunities of citizens of the United States; nor shall any State deprive any person of life, liberty, or property, without due process of law; nor deny to any person within its jurisdiction the equal protection of the laws.

Answers to Problems

Answer to Problem 1

This introductory exercise is designed to illustrate:

A.   the pervasiveness of law;

B.   that the law concerns both civil and criminal matters; and

C.   the positive nature of law—that is, most laws are protective, not punitive.

There is an infinite set of possible answers to this problem. The following are listed for purposes of illustration.

Activity	Laws	Type of Law
1. Sorting mail	Cost of postage	Federal
	Rules on opening and reading mail	U.S. Constitution and agency rules
	Rules on obscenity	Court-made laws and agency rules
2. Taking count	Time count taken	Agency Rules
	Escaped inmates	State law; agency rules
3. Feeding residents	Quality of food	Constitution; federal and state law; health codes
	Food additives	Federal agency
	Nutrition content	Federal agency; court-made law
	Religious diets	Constitutional and court-made law
	Health diets	Constitutional law and court-made law

Answer to Problem 2

A. Your opinion will form your answer to this question. The arguments for convicting them of murder include: they violated the law to which they are subject, and no legal defenses apply; people who take the life of another are guilty of murder; any mitigating circumstances will be considered at sentencing but are not relevant to the issue of guilt. The arguments against convicting them include: the law did not apply to them, since they were their own society; the law of survival is a higher law; the sailors had the defense of mental insanity; while a contract to commit a crime is illegal, their agreement formed the law of their own society.

B. This question simply points out that a middle ground to answering this problem would be to prosecute and convict but then to sentence the person to a light sentence (probation) because of the mitigating circumstances.

C. Some would say that this boat was like a correctional institution, where people are isolated and are forced to make their own rules to survive. In an institution, however, one often has two sets of rules: unwritten ones developed by the inmates and rules—both written and unwritten—developed by the administration and correctional personnel. Some might feel that the question of whether society's laws, such as constitutional rights, should be enforced in a prison is similar to the question of whether society's law prohibiting homicide should be enforced in the shipwrecked sailor case.

As mentioned in chapter 1, this is an actual case, *Regina v. Dudley and Stephens* (1884), where the people involved were tried and sentenced to death in England. The Queen, however, later reduced the sentence to six months' imprisonment.

Answer to Problem 3

A. In 1965, the District Court ruled that corporal punishment was permissible, but officials were required to develop written rules to explain what offenses could be punished by whipping and how much punishment was permitted. The District Court in 1967 again upheld corporal punishment. In 1968, the U.S. Court of Appeals, 8th Circuit, reversed this decision.

B. In 1965, the District Court ruled that corporal punishment was permissible, basing its decision on two Supreme Court decisions from other states. These decisions permitted use of the strap and said most courts that had decided the issue agreed it was not cruel and unusual punishment. The decision was binding only on the parties in the 1965 case. In 1968, the U.S. Court of Appeals reversed the District Court decision and ruled that corporal punishment was not permissible in prisons.

C. The District Court in the 1967 case based its decision on the 1965 case and on the historical viewpoint that corporal punishment and use of the strap, standing alone, did not constitute cruel and unusual punishment. The court could have ruled differently.

D. This court set a new precedent based on changed views and rejected the arguments used to back up the prior cases. The Court of Appeals is a higher court than the District Court and is not required to follow the lower court's decisions. Nor are decisions from courts of other states binding in this court, because federal courts are considered higher than state courts in resolving constitutional issues and because state courts are a separate system apart from the federal court system.

E. No. The case only decided the issue of corporal punishment and did not deal with the other circumstances involving use of force. As can be seen in chapter 2, correctional personnel do have the right to use force under certain circumstances, although when and how much depend on local laws and rules.

F. A prison might try to do this, but because many courts have cited the 1968 case favorably, it is likely that the U.S. Supreme Court ultimately would rule against the prison. It is also possible that an inmate who received corporal punishment would win a suit for damages against both the institution and the correctional personnel who administered it.

Answer to Problem 4

A. The suit is a civil one. In a criminal suit, the government (federal, state, county, or city) starts the action against a person or organization and claims that a particular criminal law has been violated. In a civil suit, a person, organization, or the government brings an action seeking either money damages or a court order. For example, in this case it might order the city either to make repairs or close down the facility.

B. This suit can be brought in either state or federal court. In order for the federal court to have jurisdiction of the case, there must be a "federal issue." In this case, that issue would be that the conditions of the facility violated the Constitution's ban on cruel and unusual punishment or the due process ban on punishment of pretrial detainees. As a practical matter, the federal court might be more inclined toward granting relief to the inmates than the state court. In the past, federal judges seemed to rule more frequently in the inmates' favor in suits by inmates, though some state courts are beginning to take a more active role in this area.

C. 1.   The Eighth Amendment's ban on cruel and unusual punishment and the due process clause of the U.S. Constitution

2.   State constitution's ban on cruel and unusual punishment and due process clause

3.   State and local laws and/or regulations on fire safety, jail regulations, and building and health codes

4.   Professional correctional standards, which are not law, may also be used to judge the legality of particular conditions.

D.   Yes. Attorneys for both sides will argue how court-made law from their own and other states should be considered by the judge in deciding the case in their favor. In this case, other cases involving jail conditions will be cited by both sides.

E.   The court could find the plaintiffs entitled to no relief and dismiss the case.

The court could find the plaintiffs entitled to relief and do any or all of the following:

1.   award money damages;

2.   enjoin the jail officials from operating the jail in this manner;

3.   appoint an expert (master) to oversee the running of the jail;

4.   release all inmates from the jail or transfer them to other institutions and order the building closed;

5.   set up a timetable of schedule changes, holding the officials in contempt if they fail to meet the schedule; and/or

6.   make defendants pay for plaintiffs' attorneys' fees.

F. 1.   If the court orders changes to be made, it is up to the legislature to appropriate this money. The legislature cannot be specifically ordered by the court to set aside monies for the jail because of the separation-of-powers doctrine, but a number of courts have created pressure that led to legislative appropriations. The agency that runs the jail will be responsible for implementing any court order in the case.

2.   The court may keep jurisdiction over the case to see that its orders are being followed and that conditions improve. Officials may be held in contempt by the court if changes are not made.

Answer to Problem 5

A.   This question calls for your opinion. As standards have been developed by a number of different groups, this process has been criticized for not taking into account views other than those of the group that has written them. (For example, some correctional administrators have criticized the American Bar Association for developing its standards based mainly on the views of lawyers and giving little consideration to the experience of those who work full-time in corrections.) The reader should decide whether each of the groups listed in Problem 5 has a right to have input into new standards and if each will add something to such a process.

B. This is also a question calling for an opinion. One advantage of mandatory standards is the resulting national uniformity that might make it clear to correctional personnel, lawyers, inmates, and judges what should take place in institutions; this, in turn, might result in more equal treatment of both correctional administrators and inmates nationwide. Disadvantages include the common belief that law enforcement is best decided on a state or local level and that, under our system of federal-state government, this has been expressly left to the states. Many believe the federal government has exceeded its power in local affairs and that this is bad in corrections and in other areas. Others object because they feel mandatory national standards do not allow for the real differences and needs of local communities—for example, rural versus urban settings.

C. You may answer this question with your opinion. An advantage of using standards is that correctional personnel and others may have spent considerable time trying to develop "reasonable" standards for an institution to follow and that this will prevent judges from making unrealistic demands on correctional personnel. Disadvantages may be that the standards will not be appropriate for the institution involved in the case and that local correctional personnel may not have been involved in drawing up the standards or may not have known of them before the case.

Answer to Problem 6

A. Though Officer Lewis may have violated his institution's rules by being abusive and, therefore, could be subject to discipline, Inmate Frank has committed a criminal assault as well as broken institutional rules. Officer Lewis under regulation II–A–1b seems to have properly defended himself against physical assault.

B. Physical force may be used here to enforce regulation II–A–1e. However, this is subject to the requirement that the minimum force necessary be used. A push that is hard enough to cause the inmate to smash into the wall is clearly excessive and could subject the officer to a civil lawsuit.

C. While Marshall may use force to enforce institutional rules, the use of force to punish an inmate for breaking the rules is forbidden.

D. Use of chemical agents is permitted to prevent an act that could result in death or severe bodily harm to the person himself or to others or to prevent serious damage to property. However, it should only be used if it is the minimum force necessary; that does not appear to be the case here. If Green was in isolation and could have been controlled by officers in some other manner, the use of tear gas was unnecessary. These facts were taken from a Virginia case, Greear v. Loving, 538 F.2d 578 (4th Cir.1976), where the Court said he would have a constitutional violation, if he was able to prove his case.

E. Physical force may be used to enforce regulations and to prevent a riot. The minimum-force requirement may mean that, in this case, the inmate should have been moved to a segregation area. This is what occurred in the actual case, Landman v. Royster, 333 F.Supp. 621 (E.D. Va.1971), where the court held that tear gas should not be used to subdue a man who did not pose a serious threat to others.

Answer to Problem 7

A. At this point, Burke probably may not shoot the inmate because he is not sure it is a weapon, but he must make some effort to warn the officer.

B. and **C.** If an officer is reasonably sure an inmate has a deadly weapon and that deadly force is necessary to prevent its use, deadly force may be used. Institutional rules may restrict this further.

Answer to Problem 8

In most states, officers may not shoot an escaping inmate unless the inmate is a convicted felon. In some states, any escaping inmate may be fired at for purposes of stopping the escape. Local rules may also spell out specific procedures to follow, such as issuing verbal warnings to halt or possibly firing a warning shot if this would not be dangerous under the circumstances. If your state court ruled that *Tennessee v. Garner* applies to prisons, it is arguable that, unless an officer in a tower knows the inmate is dangerous, he or she cannot shoot.

Answer to Problem 9

Modern correctional theories suggest that mediation and negotiation should be attempted before deadly force is used. However, if the emergency nature of the situation makes less violent means impossible, deadly force may be used.

Answer to Problem 10

The officer may be liable for damages for his negligent shooting. He may have committed the civil tort of battery. The U.S. Supreme Court said this use of force would not amount to a constitutional violation, in Whitley v. Albers, __ U.S. __, 106 S.Ct. 1078 (1986). The warden or person responsible for weapons training or the state or local government unit may also be liable for failing to train the officer properly under the theory of vicarious liability. An increased number of cases in recent years has raised failure-to-train issues, especially involving use of weapons, chemicals, and so on.

Answer to Problem 11 ◆ Supervisory Liability Case Studies

Case 1: This is based on Moon v. Winfield, 383 F.Supp. 31 (N.D.Ill. 1974). In that case, the court held that the police chief had an affirmative duty to act to protect the public from a known risk. He had the authority to suspend the officer indefinitely while seeking his discharge or to assign him to other duties. While it is true that he is only required to act in a reasonable manner, under the facts of this case, it was possible that a jury could find that the chief unreasonably failed to fulfill his duties in light of the information he had before him. Therefore, his failure to suspend or reassign could provide the affirmative link between the supervisor and the subordinate.

Case 2: Decision: warden liable; commissioner not liable. There was sufficient evidence from which to conclude that the warden must have actually known or should have known of the strip-cell conditions at the time in question. He made only rare visits to the segregation cells. As a result, even if he did not know the conditions there, his failure to exercise his responsibility for and be familiar with the treatment of inmates led to the conditions in question. Thus, he could be responsible for the "natural consequences of his actions."

While the commissioner could be held to know of the conditions in the strip cell, since he received a letter from the inmate, his actions in sending it to the warden were certainly reasonable and in no way reckless conduct on his part. The outcome would have been different if it could be shown that the commissioner was aware of the warden's total disregard for those conditions. Wright v. McMann, 460 F.2d 126 (2d Cir.1972).

Case 3: Decision: not liable. In a large institution, officials must necessarily delegate the operational responsibility for the reception, care, detention, and discharge of the inmates. They are entitled to have helpers, and once they have established—which they must—a system that eliminates as effectively as possible the hazard of mistakes, they may depend on their subordinates.

There was no evidence, such as prior errors by Choate, that would have required the defendants to doubt the assurances of the timekeeper and make a personal investigation of their own. Williams v. Anderson, 599 F.2d 923 (10th Cir.1979).

Case 4: Decision: warden and director liable. The Court of Appeals upheld an award of $32,500 against a warden, the director, the secretary of corrections, and two officers. The damages included $500 in compensatory damages against each and then punitive damages against each ranging from $10,000 to $1,000. It ruled that it was inconceivable that administrators with the statutory responsibility for enacting rules for the treatment of inmates would be unaware of a practice as rampant and as widely approved of as the use of water hoses against securely confined inmates.

Despite this awareness, they provided little or no direction to their subordinates concerning the appropriateness of the practice or the safeguards that should be followed to protect the inmates from excessive force and injury. They failed to act in the face of known risk, and the inmate's injuries were a natural consequence of their failure to act. Slakan v. Porter, 737 F.2d 368 (4th Cir.1984), cert. denied sub. nom. Reed v. Slakan, 470 U.S. 1035, 105 S.Ct. 1413 (1985).

Case 5: Decision: liable. In Grandstaff v. City of Borger, 767 F.2d 161 (5th Cir.1985), the Circuit Court of Appeals found that the chief was liable for failure to initiate departmental changes following the reckless shooting death caused by police officers. The acts of abuse proved the night of the shooting indicated a disposition to disregard human life and safety so prevalent as to be a policy or custom. The disposition of the chief of police may be inferred from his conduct after the shooting. So the subsequent acceptance of dangerous recklessness by a policymaker tends to prove his preexisting disposition and policy. The jury was entitled to infer that the conduct on the ranch demonstrated police-force policy approved by its policymaker, both before and after the shooting.

Answer to Problem 12

The court in this case, *Holda v. Kane County,* Cir. C., Kane Co., Ill. (1977), held the county liable for gross negligence, finding that conditions in the jail facilitated the attack. Punitive damages of $500,000 and $175,000 in compensatory damages were awarded. It is also possible that the jailer in charge of the institution and/or the officers on duty might be liable in a situation of this kind.

Answer to Problem 13

In this case, *Cottrell, Admin. v. Hawaii,* (1975), the court did not hold the state liable since it found that Gomez's own aggressive behavior was the cause of his death. A prevalent legal theory is that persons should not benefit from their own wrongdoing. However, it is possible that if an institution or individual was clearly responsible for allowing a gun to be brought in, liability might be found.

Answer to Problem 14

The court awarded a $1,095,000 trust fund payable from the state to compensate for the losses to the boy, his mother, and his father. Figueroa v. Hawaii, 61 Hawaii 369, 604 P.2d 1198 (1979).

Answer to Problem 15 (Role-play)

There is no definite answer for how to classify Beam. To a certain extent, it may depend on how he acts at the hearing and how he answers questions posed by the committee. The overall goal of the roleplay is to emphasize the duty institutions have to protect their inmates and to show how many factors must be considered in classification decisions. It also should be noted that officials or the institution may be held liable if such factors are not considered.

Factors the committee should consider at the hearing and in their decision include the following.

1. His crime may subject him to abuse from other inmates.

2. He has had experience in machine-shop work but will be restricted from working if he is placed in maximum security.

3. There is a possible danger from the other inmates if he is placed in medium security.

4. There is the danger of suicide if he is placed in minimum security.

Answer to Problem 16

In this hypothetical case, there was a direct violation of the jail's rule by a correctional officer. This negligence is directly connected to the escape, and the injury would likely be considered a "probable and foreseeable consequence" of the act. If there is no state immunity law, the officer might be held liable in this situation. Knowledge by the officials of the officer's frequent acts of negligence and their failure to take any action might also result in holding them personally liable.

Answer to Problem 17

A. In Johnson v. State of California, 69 Cal.2d 782, 73 Cal.Rptr 240, 447 P.2d 352 (1968), the California Supreme Court ruled that the state had to inform Mrs. Johnson of any matter that its agents knew or should have known that might endanger the Johnson family. As the party placing the youth with Mrs. Johnson, the state had a relationship to her that created a duty to warn of latent dangerous qualities suggested by the parolee's history or character.

B. This landmark case, Tarasoff v. Regents of University of California, 17 Cal.3d 425, 131 Cal.Rptr. 14, 551 P.2d 334 (1976), in which the California Supreme Court ruled that therapists had a duty to warn either the endangered party or others who should reasonably expect to be notified. In this case, a special relationship existed between the therapist and the patient that supported an affirmative duty for the benefit of third parties—here, Ms. Tarasoff. She was the known and specifically foreseeable and identifiable victim of the patient's threats and was entitled to have reasonable steps taken for her protection.

C. In Thompson v. County of Alameda, 27 Cal.3d 741, 167 Cal.Rptr. 70, 614 P.2d 728 (1980), the California Supreme Court ruled that there was no special relationship since there was no foreseeable or readily identifiable target of the delinquent's threat that he would, if released, take the life of a young child residing in that particular neighborhood. His threat was not specific enough. Therefore, there was no duty to warn the parents of the deceased boy, the parents of other neighborhood children, the police, or the delinquent's mother of the delinquent's threat.

D. In Davidson v. City of Westminster, 32 Cal.3d 197, 185 Cal.Rptr. 252, 649 P.2d 894 (1982), the California Supreme Court ruled that there was no duty of care based upon a special relationship between the officers and the assailant. The officers' proximity to an assailant, even with knowledge of his assaultive tendencies or status as a felon, does not establish a relationship imposing a duty to control the assailant. While Mrs. Davidson was a reasonably foreseeable victim, that was not enough to establish a special relationship as she was not dependent upon the police for protection. This was the case because the officers did not create the peril to Mrs. Davidson; she was unaware of their presence and did not specifically rely on them for protection. Their conduct did not increase the risk that would have existed in their absence.

E. J.A. Meyers & Co. v. Los Angeles County Probation Department, 78 Cal.App.3d 309, 144 Cal.Rptr. 186 (2d District, Div. 5 1978) ruled that, where the probation department did not place the probationer with the employer or direct him in his employment activities, there was no reliance or a special relationship.

F. Johnson v. County of Los Angeles, 191 Cal.Rptr. 704, 143 Cal.App. 3d 298 (App.2d Dist., Div. 7 1983) ruled the sheriff had a special relationship to the decedent and his wife that gave him a duty to warn the wife before releasing the husband.

Answer to Problem 18

In this case, Smith v. Miller, 241 Iowa 625, 40 N.W.2d 597 (1950), the state court cited this as a factor for the jury to consider in deciding whether the sheriff should be held liable for the injuries to the inmates. Obviously, whoever was responsible for the placement of the key and correctional officer might be held liable. It would have to be proven that a "reasonable" correctional officer would not have placed an officer so far away and that the injury could have been prevented if the officer were closer.

Answer to Problem 19

The facts given are those of Bryan v. Jones, 530 F.2d 1210 (5th Cir. 1976), where it was decided that the jury should be allowed to consider whether the sheriff was acting in good faith when he relied on the District Attorney's Office notice that the imprisonment was legal. If so, the jailer would not be liable. The right to raise this defense in a Section 1983 Civil Rights Act case presented a technical legal issue, and the court said: "In a case such as this one, where there is no discretion and relatively little time pressure, the jailer will be held to a high level of reasonableness as to his own actions. If he negligently establishes a record keeping system in which errors of this kind are likely, he will be held liable. But if the errors take place outside of his realm of responsibility, he cannot be found liable because he has acted reasonably and in good faith." Consequently, the case was remanded for a new trial, at which time the defendant sheriff was allowed to present a good-faith defense to liability.

Answer to Problem 20

In this case, DiFebo v. Keve, 395 F.Supp. 1350 (D.Del.1975), the federal court said that the facts did not constitute a claim under Section 1983 (not "deliberate indifference" as required by *Estelle v. Gamble,* see chapter 3). But the court said the facts would be sufficient to establish a negligence claim under state tort law. If a state court found that the warden or other personnel had been negligent in not replacing the glasses and that this caused further damage, the individuals responsible and/or the local government unit might be liable.

Answer to Problem 21

A. Reasons against this include:

    1.   Cost. It is doubtful any insurance company would agree to insure any injury received for any reason.

    2.   The limit on any given inmate's claim would be less than the inmate might be able to recover from a court case.

    3.   Officers no longer fearing personal liability will have less reason to respect the rights of inmates.

    4.   Injury claims by one inmate often raise questions about overall conditions of prisons or jails, and courts order broader relief.

    5.   It takes the court out of contact with conditions within the correctional system.

B.   This asks for your opinion. In addition to the points just listed, the same positive and negative factors pertaining to workers' compensation outside of prison apply: relief in shorter time and relief regardless of fault versus smaller recoveries. Also, because inmates have a harder time getting counsel, more cases might be remedied under workers' compensation.

C.   In Meredith v. Workers' Compensation Appeals Bd., 19 Cal.3d 777, 140 Cal.Rptr. 314, 567 P.2d 746 (1977), the court found that the system did not violate the inmates' rights in this case, but future cases might be decided differently.

Answer to Problem 22

A.   Diane Rawlinson succeeded in her challenge to this regulation. She first had to show that the rule had a discriminatory impact on women, which she did through statistics showing that many more women than men were shorter than five feet, two inches. The correctional institution then had the burden (which, in this case, it failed to carry) of showing that the height and weight requirements were necessary for performing the job of correctional officers. Dothard v. Rawlinson, 433 U.S. 321, 97 S.Ct. 2720 (1977).

B.   This claim is proper under the law, but if the correctional institution is able to show that the test was professionally developed and was not designed to discriminate and that it was related to the requirements of the job, it would fall within the exception to the law and be permitted.

In Aguilera v. Cook County Police and Corrections Merit Board, 760 F.2d 844 (7th Cir.1985), a federal appeals court ruled that a high school education was a reasonable qualification to require of corrections officers even though the requirement had a disproportionate impact on Hispanics. A Hispanic proved that 70 percent of the white residents in the county age twenty-five and older had a high school education compared to only 35 percent of Hispanics.

The county then proved that a high school education bore a demonstrable relationship to successful performance of the job. Police officers are required to have such a diploma, and corrections work presents as great a challenge. Additionally, in 1984 inmates filed 19,000 civil rights suits against the corrections agencies. Officers are required to take college-level courses, and high school diplomas are required for college. ACA standards also called for officers to be able to interpret and implement court decisions.

C. The courts have not ruled on this particular issue. A court faced with the problem would have to decide which "right" was more important in this situation—privacy for inmates or no discrimination for officers. Case law trends indicate greater protection is afforded job rights over privacy. This case points out the problems a court must deal with in trying to accommodate the conflicting rights of more than one group.

Answer to Problem 23

A. This calls for an opinion. Some reasons for and against it appear in the text.

B. Those in favor of unions would probably argue that each of these problems or complaints could be resolved better if correctional administrators, state officials, legislators, and the public were able to hear the views of correctional officers. Unions might use methods such as press releases, position papers, meetings, negotiations, strikes or slowdowns, picketing, and lobbying to express their viewpoints on these issues.

C. Those against unions argue that the viewpoint of correctional personnel can be included without the expense of unions or the antagonism that might result. Unions, they argue, may create an adversarial relationship and undermine morale and discipline. They may also argue that strikes and slowdowns can be very dangerous. Additionally, officers may be divided in their loyalties between union and nonunion members; this has the potential of causing problems.

Answer to Problem 24

Reasons for Limiting Rights in a
Correctional Institution:

1. Deterrence
2. Punishment
3. Rehabilitation
4. Internal order of institution
5. Cost
6. Security
7. Administrative
   inconvenience

Reasons against Limiting Rights in a
Correctional Institution:

1. Rehabilitation
2. Constitutional rights still
   exist.
3. Loss of freedom is
   sufficient punishment.

Note that these may not be accepted by the court as reasons for restricting the rights of inmates and that some of the reasons given do not
apply to pretrial inmates.

Answer to Problem 25

Some argue that pretrial detainees should have more rights since
they are presumed innocent of any crime, and, in many cases, those
in jail would be on the street enjoying the full rights of ordinary
citizens if they had had the money to pay bond. Others argue,
however, that the vast majority are guilty, and it is too difficult to
provide rights in an institution. Others justify restricting rights in
the interest of security or orderly functioning of the institution,
which the U.S. Supreme Court has permitted. In *Bell v. Wolfish* (cited
in the student text), the Supreme Court's test for pretrial inmates
was whether they were being "punished." The Court contrasted this
with the test for convicted inmates, which is whether the punishment is "cruel and unusual."

Answer to Problem 26

A. The First Amendment protects you in your phone conversation
unless you are making a threat on the President's life. You cannot be
convicted of a crime for saying the President is a bum. However,
time, place, and manner in regard to free speech may be regulated. In
all likelihood, you could stand on a park bench and state your criti-
cisms of the President, unless you drew a large crowd that caused a
disturbance, blocked traffic, and so on. Blocking traffic will generally not be tolerated, nor can you incite a riot; you could be arrested
and convicted. In some instances, a permit may be required to speak
in a public place.

B.   Private writings may be kept at home with no problem. If you said the same things to a crowd on a street corner or on television, the test is likely to be whether there was a clear and present danger that the crowd or viewing audience would be incited to use force and violence. If there were no such danger, the speech would be protected, and, if you were arrested, you would not be convicted. To be convicted, you would have to make an actual "call to action" rather than a theoretical statement.

C.   The wearing of armbands is symbolic speech, which the Supreme Court said, in Tinker v. Des Moines Indep. Community School Dist., 393 U.S. 503, 89 S.Ct. 733 (1969), was protected speech. Students could not be expelled or suspended unless the wearing of armbands resulted in a "substantial disruption" of the educational process.

D.   The government may not censor the mail. If you take action or take part in a conspiracy, you may have broken the law and may be subject to criminal prosecution.

Answer to Problem 27 (Role-play)

A.   Yes, Sostre v. McGinnis, 442 F.2d 178 (2d Cir.1971) held that punishing Sostre for putting his thoughts on paper without giving him prior warning and without knowing whether he intended to distribute them violated his First Amendment rights. (This case should not be cited in the role-play but could be discussed after arguments are brought out on both sides and a decision is made.)

B.   The court did not resolve this issue, but it did state that, in the absence of arbitrariness or discrimination, if the warden had chosen to *confiscate* the writings rather than to punish Sostre, the court would probably not have overturned the warden's judgment. The warden, however, would have to show there was a legitimate governmental interest unrelated to the suppression of speech—for example, that possession of the writings would be likely to result in circulation among other inmates, which in turn would be likely to subvert prison discipline.

C.   The court said that a rule forbidding Sostre to hand out such writings to other inmates would be justified.

Answer to Problem 28

A.   Although the Supreme Court has not ruled on this issue, an inmate would probably be protected by the First Amendment for verbal criticism of a jail's operation. However, reasonable limits on activities that pose a danger to prison security would be allowed. Therefore, seeking out other inmates to discuss his views, in a way that would cause a security problem, could probably be limited if not completely stopped.

B.   This answer is subject to local rules. Courts have differed on the extent of a prisoner's right to possess materials and magazines with sexual content. Some courts have held that regulations giving broad authority on this matter to prison officials are too "vague" or "overbroad." Other courts have banned magazines that are clearly obscene under the Supreme Court standard. Courts differ on whether *Playboy* or *Hustler* are obscene, though most have ruled they are not.

In Hunter v. Koehler, 618 F.Supp. 13 (W.D.Mich.1984), a federal court approved a prison policy precluding inmates from receiving materials describing or showing acts of homosexuality, sadism, violent sexual practices, and/or unlawful sexual behavior, as well as nude snapshots taken with home cameras. This was related to legitimate security concerns of security and rehabilitation. The fact that inmates were afforded an opportunity for an administrative hearing to challenge rejection of materials was viewed as very important by the court.

C.   The institution's reasons for taking it away might include preventing escape plans, or prison officials might argue that it contains information on the construction of weapons or the dismantling of existing security systems. These legitimate security concerns would permit the opening, reading, and censoring of incoming unofficial mail. A pretrial detainee's mail right depends on the institution's rules and local court cases. Some courts have only permitted the opening of mail to inspect for contraband and have said it cannot be read. Mail most often protected has been that from attorneys or courts. The issue of whether mail to and from family or friends may be restricted has not yet been settled by the Supreme Court.

Answer to Problem 29

A.   In Abdullah v. Kinnison, 769 F.2d 345 (6th Cir.1985), the 6th Circuit Court of Appeals ruled that, because restriction of the robes to chapel use was an intelligent effort to use the least restrictive means necessary for security, it was constitutional.

B.   In Brown v. Johnson, 743 F.2d 408 (6th Cir.1984), cert. denied Inosencio v. Johnson, 469 U.S. 1215, 105 S.Ct. 1190 (1985), the Federal Court of Appeals upheld a decision by the Michigan Department of Corrections to deny homosexual inmates the right to worship as a group. Prison officials are afforded discretion in deciding which groups should be allowed to meet within prison walls, and here officials proved there was a potential danger. Sufficient evidence was presented to indicate a strong correlation between inmate homosexuality and prison violence, including at least twenty-six incidents of serious violence of which three were homicides. The ban on group worship was designed to decrease the contact between dangerous inmates and inmates attending the services.

C. In Cruz v. Beto, 405 U.S. 319, 92 S.Ct. 1079 (1972), the Supreme Court ruled that a Buddhist inmate could not be prevented from using the chapel or writing his religious supervisor. If there are enough Buddhist inmates, an institution might be required to pay for a Buddhist chaplain. The courts have not yet dealt with this issue.

D. In Banks v. Havener, 234 F.Supp. 27 (E.D.Va.1964), an inmate was allowed to wear a religious medal, even though jewelry had been banned from prisoners in other cases for security reasons. A later case Monroe v. Bombard, 422 F.Supp. 211 (S.D.N.Y.1976) held that a "no beard" rule violated the religious freedoms of Sunni Muslims in New York because their religion advised them to wear beards. However, other courts might find security problems resulting from religious jewelry or wearing beards to be more important than the right to religious freedom.

E. Most cases disallowing services for inmates in segregation have been upheld. However, some courts have encouraged institutions to find alternate methods to afford religious practice for those in solitary confinement.

Answer to Problem 30

Many believe there are several benefits to permitting inmates to practice their religion. They argue that it encourages self-reflection and a desire to change past behavior, that it gives a sense of meaning to an otherwise meaningless life, and that support from the religious community may assist the inmate by requiring discipline and constructive use of time. On the whole, religion may enhance the atmosphere within the institution.

Answer to Problem 31

Assuming the institution decides this is a religion and not merely a cover-up for what otherwise would be impermissible activities, the following provisions and restrictions would apply.

A. It could be argued that paying for any chaplain may be unconstitutional because it is establishing religion, but courts have not as yet dealt with either this issue or the issue of paying for chaplains of certain religions.

B. Institutions do not have to provide pizza as communion because to do so may constitute unconstitutional establishment of religion and/or because such a practice may be costly or an administrative burden. It could also be argued that pizza for use in religious services is an obviously unreasonable request for a religion as was decided in the *Theriault* case cited on p. 83, when inmates requested steak and wine.

C.   The institution must provide use of the chapel to all religions if requested, unless a legitimate state interest in security or maintaining discipline is presented. Although it may not discriminate or prohibit practice of religions with smaller congregations, the institution is permitted to take the size of any religious congregation into account when giving preference in terms of scheduling.

D.   If the institution permits other religions to hold special services, it may not be able to justify preventing the members of the Church of the New Faith from having a similar service. If no such services are permitted to any religious group, the warden would be justified in denying this request.

E.   Unless the institution can show some threat to security, the inmates will be allowed to circulate their rules. This would be especially true if other groups are allowed to circulate their rules.

F.   The Constitution does not require complete privacy during their religious services. Even if inmates argued that their religion required privacy, the duty of correctional officers to insure safety of the inmates would outweigh the religious right.

Answer to Problem 32

In re Reynolds, 25 Cal.3d 131, 157 Cal.Rptr. 892, 599 P.2d 86 (1979) is the basis for this problem. In that case:

A.   the court found that wearing the union button was "speech" as protected by the Constitution; and

B.   where the department had not claimed past or future disruption from wearing the button, the inmates were allowed to obtain and wear buttons.

Answer to Problem 33

A.   Citizens have First Amendment freedoms of speech and the press that protect these actions.

B.   Freedom of the press is the First Amendment right involved. However, few cases have been decided on this issue. One case, *Kirkland v. Hardy* (U.S. District Court for D.C., 1972), did result in a consent decree allowing the newspaper to be published if no names of correctional employees were used. It is probably a valid assumption that circulating material in the prison and naming correctional officials may properly be banned. Some courts have upheld the right of inmates to publish criticism of prison officials, advocate legitimate use of prison grievance procedures, or urge inmates to contact public representatives, as long as the publications don't attempt to break down prison discipline or cause disruptions. Guajardo v. Estelle, 580 F.2d 748 (5th Cir.1978), supplemented 568 F.Supp. 1354 (S.D.Tex.1983).

C. Questions of freedoms of speech and the press are raised here. The *Saxbe* case and the *Houchins* case cited in the student text allow prison and jail officials to provide no greater right to individual interviews with inmates by the press than the general public has. Therefore, the paper could correspond with him, and if the inmates have a right to visit with the general public, they may also talk to the press.

Answer to Problem 34

The Court, in Storms v. Coughlin, 600 F.Supp. 1214 (S.D.N.Y.1984), ruled this procedure violated the Fourth Amendment ban on unreasonable searches. It stated that the potential for abuse was great, since, as long as the commander is potentially aware of the name of the prisoner he is choosing, he may, consciously or unconsciously, choose less-favored inmates.

Answer to Problem 35

A. No strip search can be performed. There is no reasonable belief to search, because there is no significant opportunity for introduction of contraband. The officer may conduct a pat-down search, and, depending upon what shows up, reasonable belief may be established for a strip search.

B. Yes, the officer may conduct a body cavity search of the mouth, since the officer would have a reasonable belief.

C. Yes, this is a reasonable belief, as the inmate may be concealing some kind of illegal contraband.

D. Yes, this is a reasonable belief for the same reason as in answer 3.

E. Hill v. Bogans, 735 F.2d 391 (10th Cir.1984) involved a similar set of facts. The Court of Appeals ruled that his rights were violated and that he was entitled to a money judgment. The court noted that the arrestee's offenses are not offenses associated with the concealment of weapons or contraband in a body cavity.

F. Yes, this is reasonable belief, as the officer has reliable information to go on plus suspicious activity by the inmate.

G. No, this is not a situation where the inmate has a significant opportunity to receive contraband, since the individual is searched before leaving. If there were information to lead an officer to have a reasonable belief that a specific inmate had obtained contraband from the vehicle or from other persons, a strip search could be conducted.

H. Yes, this is a significant opportunity to receive contraband.

I. No. This is not a significant opportunity to receive contraband. However, if the officer had a reasonable belief that a certain inmate has received contraband during a noncontact visit, a strip search could be conducted.

J. Yes, this may be a significant opportunity to receive contraband; there have been some cases of attorneys smuggling in contraband. In New York, a strip search may be conducted after attorney visits. However, in Iowa, Goff v. Nix, 626 F.Supp. 736 (S.D.Iowa 1984), the District Court banned the state prison from conducting visual anal and body-cavity searches before and after visits with attorneys, legal interns with notarized letters of introduction from a licensed attorney, clergy, the prison chaplain, or representatives of the prison ombudsman's office.

K. No, since the inmate is leaving without supervision, there is no significant opportunity to receive contraband, nor is there reasonable belief to think the inmate has contraband.

L. Yes, under certain circumstances. One federal case held:

1.   If the inmate has notice of the date of the trip;

2.   If the inmate has a history of escape, abscond or attempts to escape or abscond; or

3.   Additionally, if, during a supervised outside trip, the escorting officer loses sight of the inmate or his hand movements and the officer believes the inmate has contraband, the inmate may be strip searched upon return to the facility.

M. Yes, during a routine block search, a strip search and inspection of the mouth, ears, hair, hands, armpits, and feet may be conducted. Yes, if there is a major threat to security, an entire search, including strip searches of all inmates, may be conducted.

N. No, medical personnel, unlike correctional officers, may perform opposite-sex searches. In emergencies, officers of the opposite sex could conduct such a strip search if delay in getting a same-sex officer would pose a security problem.

O. One, unless a supervisor is necessary. Exceptions are for emergencies and group searches or where there is reason to believe there will be active resistence to a strip search.

P.   Yes, if partitions or curtains separate each area and inmates from each other, if area is adequately clean and heated, and if inmates can keep their clothes off the floor.

Answer to Problem 36

A. On Street	B. In Jail
Meet with attorney and tell all.	Meet with attorney and tell all, but attorney has more difficult time since attorney must come to jail.
Line up witnesses to establish alibi defense.	Meet with jailhouse lawyer and receive help.
Try to find person who did it if you are innocent.	Talk to family and friends to get them to line up witnesses for alibi and to find out who did it.
Talk to witnesses.	
Suggest attorney file motion to dismiss case or motion to suppress identification.	Suggest attorney file motion to dismiss or suppress identification.
Do research in law library to assist attorney.	Do research in law library.
Line up character witnesses and letters for sentencing if convicted.	Write letter or ask friends to line up witnesses and letters for sentencing.
Live with family.	
Maintain job or find employment, which will more likely lead to probation if you are convicted.	

Note that all items in list (A) can be done by someone on the street (perhaps with the exception of talking to the victim or other witnesses who may not cooperate), but the circumstances of being incarcerated restrict performing the steps in list (B).

C.   A police officer could not stop you from doing any of the things in (A). Jail authorities cannot stop you from doing the things in (B), but they can limit your activities by regulating the time and place you do them. They can also restrict your ability to do such things as research in the law library by maintaining a less-than-adequate law-book collection or by restricting the hours of use available to you.

D.   In Williams v. Leeke, 584 F.2d 1336 (4th Cir.1978) cert. denied 442 U.S. 911, 99 S.Ct. 2825 (1979), the court found that this program violated the Sixth Amendment. The court's finding was that city jail prisoners are entitled to reasonable access to the courts and that this was not provided to a person serving a substantial sentence of confinement if, without other legal assistance, his only access to a law library was so restricted as to be meaningless.

E.   This case was consolidated for hearing with (D). The court found that if Williams were an ordinary prisoner and if the prison only provided a law library with limited access, it would be unconstitutional. However, where known security risks were given legal assistance along with library books brought to their cells, the right of access was satisfied.

F. Correctional personnel may conclude that jailhouse lawyers become too powerful within the institution and take advantage of others, that inmates frequently file frivolous and repetitive claims which require extensive time to defend, and that law libraries are too expensive to maintain, and are underused by inmates.

Answer to Problem 37

Students are free to agree or disagree with these answers given by the Supreme Court.

1. Disagree. The Supreme Court in both a jail-overcrowding case (Bell v. Wolfish, 441 U.S. 520, 99 S.Ct. 1861 (1979)) and in a prison-overcrowding case (Rhodes v. Chapman, 452 U.S. 337, 101 S.Ct. 2392 (1981)) decided that the opinions of experts do not establish what the Constitution requires. They merely present goals but are not necessarily evidence of a constitutional violation, unless the Court agrees they violate the Constitution.

2. Disagree. Given the newness of the facility and the fact that most other conditions were good, the Supreme Court ruled that the facility was not constitutionally offensive.

3. Disagree. The Supreme Court ruled that, even though double-celling may not be desirable, especially in view of cell size, the practice does not create unnecessary and wanton pain. In particular, the court noted that the facilities were exceptionally modern and functional and contained not the traditional type cells in which inmates were locked up for most of the day.

4. Disagree. In the early days of litigation involving overcrowding, many courts did use the design capacity as a guide to whether or not the institution was unconstitutionally overcrowded. However, courts now consider design capacity and square footage as only one factor to be weighed in determining whether the overcrowding is a constitutional violation.

5. Agree. The Court considers the adequacy of basic life necessities in determining whether the overcrowding is unconstitutional. Where they are adequate, there is no violation.

6. Agree. Out-of-cell time is another important factor in determining whether there is a constitutional violation.

Answer to Problem 38

A. and B.   These are both from the case of Todaro v. Ward, 431 F.Supp. 1129 (S.D.N.Y.1977) aff'd Todaro v. Coughlin, 652 F.2d 54 (2d Cir. 1981), which found these aspects of the prison medical system to violate the cruel and unusual punishment clause of the Eighth Amendment because they constituted "deliberate indifference" to the inmates' needs.

C.   The facts clearly show grounds for a Section 1983 lawsuit on grounds of cruel and unusual punishment or due process, as well as a state tort action.

Recent cases have made it clear that correctional personnel have a duty to act, if possible, to prevent such attacks. If the officer was in danger had he tried to stop it, he nevertheless should have called for help.

D.   This is the case of Bourgeois v. United States, 375 F.Supp. 133 (N.D.Tex.1974), where the inmate was able to prove a constitutional violation of the Eighth Amendment, and received $25,000 for pain and suffering and $15,000 for loss in earning capacity.

Answer to Problem 39

A.   Failure to provide medical care to this inmate could result in liability for the officer as well as for the state or municipality. To file a successful Section 1983 suit, the inmate must show the denial was the result of "deliberate indifference." A negligence or medical malpractice suit might also be filed in state court. Officers should follow the procedures in their institution for seeing a doctor, and officials should have doctors available on either a short-call basis or full-time within the institution.

B.   These are the facts in *Estelle v. Gamble,* cited in the student text, where the U.S. Supreme Court found that the situation did not give rise to a cruel and unusual punishment claim since it was not "deliberate indifference" on the part of correctional officials. The court went on to say that the inmate might file a medical malpractice suit in the state courts.

Answer to Problem 40

A.   In Kershaw v. Davis, U.S.Dist.Ct., (N.D.Pa.1977), the court found a constitutional violation for failing to provide women with work release programs. The court stated that this female had a valid claim for wages she would have earned if allowed to participate in the program.

B.   1.   The California Court of Appeals decided that there was a violation of the equal protection clause of the federal and state constitution, thus ruling in favor of the female inmates in Molar v. Gates, 98 Cal. App.3d 1, 159 Cal.Rptr. 239 (4th Dist.1979).

a.   Yes.

b.   The court ruled that the state did not have sufficient justification to treat the women differently and rejected the sheriff's arguments based on state law and the constitutional right to privacy.

Protecting women inmates from sexual assault is a critical governmental interest. However, the court found there was no logical or substantial relationship between the goal of protection and its attainment by denying female inmates the opportunity to be incarcerated in a minimum-security facility. The sheriff's real argument was the lack of money, but budgetary considerations do not justify governmental violation of equal protection.

The court was also not persuaded by the defendant's arguments against them; and that the small number of female inmates, the number of inmates needed to maintain the women's jail, and the need to run an efficient jail justify the different treatment. The number of women sentenced to jail was shown to be significant; furthermore, this is really a mask for the defense of no money.

The U.S. Constitution takes precedence over state law. The sheriff's duty to provide some separation of the sexes did not have to be violated to provide privileges to the females. Also, since the privileges provided to the males were privileges and not rights, the jail did not have to provide them to either group.

2.   The appeals court agreed with the trial court's remedy: The jail must discontinue the privileges presently extended to males or take appropriate steps to extend similar privileges to female inmates. It was important in this decision that the difference in treatment dealt with privileges, not rights. Had the difference in treatment been based on rights—for example, free speech—or on cruel and unusual punishment, the sheriff would not have had the option to discontinue the more favorable treatment of male inmates.

Answer to Problem 41

A.   The probable answer would be that you would protest such a firing. You would investigate the institution's or agency's rules regarding firing and possibly see an attorney. You should demand a hearing, where you would tell your side of the story and present evidence to refute the charges against you.

B. A permanent employee who can only be dismissed for cause in this situation would claim that his or her right to due process had been violated and that the following should be provided before dismissal:

1. an oral or written notice of charges against the employee;
2. an opportunity to have the evidence explained;
3. an opportunity to present his or her side of the story.

Answer to Problem 42

A. Where the action taken by the institution may be in retaliation for the employee's exercise of his right to form and participate in a permitted union, the courts have held that he is entitled to a hearing.

B. Firing may be a proper remedy in this case, but the doctor is probably entitled to a hearing. In one case, the court ruled that a corrections employee was denied his right to due process in a similar situation. He was denied a property interest in his job, because he had a reasonable expectation of continuing in his job as the result of a state statute allowing discharge only for just cause. Faulkner v. North Carolina Dept. of Corrections, 428 F.Supp. 100 (W.D.N.C.1977).

C. In Seales v. Malcolm, 61 A.D.2d 920, 403 N.Y.S.2d 5 (1978), the court reduced the officer's punishment from dismissal to a suspension because it found that dismissal was too great a punishment for the employee's act.

Answer to Problem 43 (Role-play)

If the role-play is enacted as described in the student text, the following legal points are illustrated.

A. When the report is read, the inmate is properly being given notice of the charges against him, but *Wolff v. McDonnell* required that inmates receive written notice at least twenty-four hours before the hearing to give them an opportunity to prepare a defense. Therefore, the request for a postponement should have been granted.

B. The denial of legal counsel was proper under *Wolff* because Gray is literate, and the issues are not so complex that a lawyer or someone substituting for a lawyer is necessary or required.

C. The board could legitimately decide not to allow cross-examination of Officer Jones if it believed this to be better for security and necessary to avoid disruption within the institution. The board has an obligation to tell its reason for denial, either here or if sued later in court.

D. The board's unwillingness to allow Gray to call Miller or hear testimony from Miller might be seen by some courts as a denial of due process. However, the U.S. Supreme Court has usually left this to the discretion of correctional officials.

E.   The board can refuse to allow the ten witnesses on grounds that they would be repetitive, and it probably could refuse to allow calling even one of them because it is not claimed that anyone saw the incident. Bias is always relevant, so perhaps one might be called.

F.   Gray can be asked to leave the room because the U.S. Supreme Court has said that correctional officials may decide that this is necessary for security in the institution. In addition, Reynolds might not be willing to testify in Gray's presence out of fear of reprisal.

Note: All the preceding answers are based on what the U.S. Supreme Court has said is the minimum due process required. However, other courts and many state and local correctional agencies have gone further and provided the right to call witnesses, to cross-examine, and to be represented by a person of the inmate's choice. These answers may be different in some areas when one refers to the local rules or court decisions.

Answer to Problem 44

A.   If an inmate is being placed in administrative segregation for a disciplinary violation, a due process hearing is required. If the officials have a nonpunitive reason—for example, the danger of a riot—then no hearing is required under the U.S. Constitution, but state laws or prison regulations may require it. Arbitrary or discriminatory use of administrative segregation can always be challenged in court.

B.   Inmates can be placed in administrative segregation for a variety of reasons, including their own protection, but there must be some opportunity for periodic review by officials of their continued confinement there.

C.   Under the U.S. Constitution, the courts have held that inmates had no right to due process hearings before transfers interstate or intrastate unless state law or prison regulations create such a liberty interest.

Answer to Problem 45

A.   Most cases are filed in federal court because federal judges have traditionally been viewed as more willing than state judges to find that the Constitution provides greater protection to inmates. Since state judges are often elected, they are seen as more closely tied to the government of that state and are viewed as less willing to take action to enforce the rights of inmates and more willing to go along with the local government.

B. While state and federal courts have the same range of remedies available (e.g., injunctions, damages), certain defenses available to correctional personnel in negligence suits in state courts are not available in federal courts (e.g., "sovereign immunity"). Moreover, attorneys may be more easily obtained in federal court by inmates since attorney's fees may be awarded in federal court without a showing of the institution's bad faith.

Answer to Problem 46

A. This was not an actual case, but courts would probably hold that correctional officials should have found a way to get him access to the law library even though he was in solitary confinement. The good faith defense would not be available to correctional officials, because the right of access to a law library or a suitable alternative was clearly established in the 1976 case of *Bounds v. Smith,* and the prison officers "reasonably should have known" about the law.

B. The fact that Williams won his release after access to the library might make him eligible for damages on the theory that he spent an extra year in prison because of the violation.

Answer to Problem 47

A correctional officer should act as a professional at all times when in contact with inmates. Although it may be difficult, the officer should ignore such a remark.

Answer to Problem 48

A. Tort Suit

   1.

Defendants	A/B	Neg.	Torts Sup. Liab.
Beam	x	x	
Grant	x	x	x
Training Off.	x	x	x
Warden	x	x	x
State	x	x	x

   2. The State's Attorney's office will clearly represent everyone but Beam. A determination would be made initially whether or not Beam was acting within the scope of his employment. Given the differing accounts of what happened, the state could not determine what happened and would be obliged to provide Beam with a defense.

However, because there may well be a conflict of interest between Beam and the state, as evidenced by the written reprimand, the state may hire independent counsel to represent Beam.

3.   Easly must prove his case. If he can successfully prove his version of the events, then he could win on the assault-and-battery and negligence-in-summoning-medical-care claims. Easly would have to prove that the state had a seriously inadequate training program to succeed on the failure-to-train claim. He would have to prove that the supervisor had reason to know that this employee was unfit for this assignment prior to this event to succeed on the negligent-assignment claim.

4.   If Easly wins, he will win money damages. On the assault-and-battery tort, he could win compensatory and punitive damages. For the negligent torts, he could probably win only compensatory damages.

5.   State law differs on its indemnification policies. A typical state tort claims law would require the state to pay for compensatory, but not punitive, damages *if* the employee was acting within the scope of employment and without fraud, corruption, or malice. If the inmate proves his claims of how the assault and battery happened, Beam will pay compensatory and punitive damages. Judgments against the supervisors, if successful, would be paid for by the state.

6.   Since this is a tort suit, Easly will pay his own attorney's fees. The attorney would probably take a percentage of the money recovered from Beam and the state.

B.   Civil Rights Violations

1.

Defendants	Constitutional Violations	
	Due Process	C & U Pun.
Beam	x	x
Foster Grant	x	x
Trainer	x	x
Warden	x	x
State	x	x

2.   The same analysis applies as in question 1.

3.   If Easly can prove his version of the events, he can establish a due process violation against Beam. The state can never be a named defendant in Section 1983 suits. In order for supervisors to be liable for constitutional violations of subordinates, there must be an affirmative link between the employee's act and the supervisor's responsibility.

If Beam were found to be negligent in the infliction of injuries, there would be no due process violation. To prove cruel and unusual punishment, Easly would have to prove deliberate indifference to serious medical needs. Insufficient facts are given to explain why the twelve-hour delay occurred.

4.   Easly would win money damages, compensatory, and perhaps punitive damages. He might also get an injunction to improve the medical-response system and to improve training programs.

5.   The same analysis applies as to question 1, subquestion e.

6.   In Section 1983 suits, the defendant must pay for Easly's attorney's fees if Easly prevails in his case.

C.   Grand jury

1.   Because no representation is permitted in grand jury proceedings, the State's Attorney will not represent him. If there are further criminal proceedings, the state will not provide representation. States do not provide representation in criminal charges.

Index

Parole System and Inmates